How To Be
A
Great
Camp Counselor

by David Burrow

McElroy Publishing
27-33 Fredonian Street • P.O. Box 488
Shirley, MA 01464

508-425-4055
800-225-0682

ISBN 0-9622191-4-2

This book is affectionately dedicated to my dear mother, Mrs. Harriot Rigor.

Table of Contents

Note: The use of "He", "his", "him", in some chapters is
          used as a grammatical neuter and is not intended to
          apply only to the male half of camp.

Acknowledgements

I am grateful to my wife, Carol, and my friend, Mrs. Beverly Crego, for repeatedly reading and correcting the manuscript. Without the dedicated effort of Jack McElroy, this book would not have come into existence. I wish to extend special thanks to Linda Slattery for her fine, original illustrations. Lastly, may the Lord bless the long hours invested by Miriam Thebeau in typing, correcting, and formatting each page.

How to Use this Book

Dear Counselor,

This is probably the most unique Camp Counselor Manual available today.

Why?

Because it is the only book that's been set up to be a pocket guide to give you quick and easy answers to a whole bunch of problems you'll probably run into here at camp.

The answers given and the methods outlined <u>WORK</u>. They've been developed over 20+ years of working with youth.

If you follow the easy instructions given in this book, you'll <u>enjoy</u> the wonderful experience of being a Camp Counselor!

Here's all you have to do...

Study the table of contents, and when you're faced with one of the problems listed there, turn to the section, read it and do what it says.

It's that simple!

When you've got free time, read over new sections and reread other sections.

You can read the book right through or jump around. It doesn't matter.

Just follow the instructions and may you have a wonderful summer with your children.

Jack McElroy, President
McElroy Publishing

1 How to Start off Right

Now you have a wonderful opportunity to be a great camp counselor.

But before I tell you how to do it, you need to know <u>why</u> it's so important.

So here goes:

1. What <u>you</u> do at camp may make the difference between a good and bad experience for your campers.

2. If you use this manual you'll be creating wonderful memories for your campers...If you don't, you'll probably turn them off to camping!

Here's how to do it the right way.

1. You're here to give your kids the best week (s) of their lives.

    Remind yourself of this daily.

2. See your job as exactly what it is, a service to children.

Being a counselor means giving, giving, giving. But did you know that as you forget about yourself and give yourself totally to your campers that you will actually get the most out of camp?

You will work harder than you do during most of the school year. Your day may start as early as 6:00 a.m. and not end until 10:30 or 11:00 p.m. But no one will be pushing or prodding you to do it.

You will be expected to be on time, to participate, to cooperate, to do your very best all the time, and all without outside reminders!

You will have the time of your life as a counselor, but when something (or a certain someone!) begins to hamper your duty to the camper, it is time to put distractions aside and get back to the real purpose of your being at camp.

3.　　　Don't worry about your shortcomings.

When you walk into camp, it may mean a whole new beginning for you. It's like a fresh start.

Are you shy?

Be more outgoing, and then take the first step by telling yourself, "Forget that shy routine; go up and talk to your campers. Find two questions to ask to get a conversation started."

Do you see yourself as a failure?   NO ONE FAILS unless he doesn't try and doesn't follow this manual.

Whatever your past, (i.e.,hang-ups, pride, wrong motives, wrong priorities, personal problems) hang it on a nail outside of camp! Remember, this can be a new beginning for you.

4.   Follow the plan your Camp Director has given you.

The Director and staff here have a purpose for everything. Hundreds of details have been thought through in advance, so go with the plan and forget the complaining.

People make this camp effective, but people can be the biggest problem too. People who don't understand or who don't have all the information may gripe, gossip, grumble, and grouch.

They get their motives twisted, so they sow discord & spread negative undercurrents.

While some people specialize in creating problems, why don't _YOU_ vow to be part of the solution.

5.   Be loyal to the Director and your supervisor.
See yourself and EVERYONE else on the camp staff
as part of the team functioning together in unity.

2 How to Succeed the First Day

Here are several basic principles for you to follow in order to get off to a good start.

As soon as a camper drives into camp, go out and greet him cheerfully and welcome him to camp. Help the camper's family feel right at home by helping them know where to park, where to go first, and so forth.

After the registration line, be available to help carry the luggage. You should be available to anyone who needs help.

Make sure to introduce yourself and help the campers learn your name. It is even more important for you to learn <u>each</u> of <u>their</u> <u>names</u>. Take the time, it's worth it.

You are needed in the cabin. As the camper comes to your "home away from home," greet him with a big smile, hello, and introductions. Let him choose his bed from those that are left; help him make it up, put away suitcases, and introduce him to all the others in the cabin.

Now you have a problem. "What do we do?" You can't leave the cabin because more are still coming through registration. Each camp should have its solutions, but here are some possibilities if you need more help.

What to Do During Registration Time

1.   Have a simple game to play in the cabin. This will be <u>needed</u> if it's raining. It can be a group game like "20 Questions" or "Guess what I'm thinking of." It can be paper and pen games like "Tic-Tac-Toe","Dot-to-Dot", or "Hang Man." Be ready with these extra resources.

2.   Send the new campers off two by two. Send the old camper with a new one. The objective is to have the "old timer" introduce the new one to all the buildings and places in camp. Of course, you are hoping that a new friendship will develop.

3.   Have a craft project ready in the cabin. Each camper could make a name tag and then wear it for two days. Make a cabin logo. Create a cabin cheer, a name, a poem, a goal for the week. Fix up the outside area of the cabin by raking, lining the path with stones, etc.

4.   If it's a teen camp, use #2 (and forget the rest). Teens will want to do little more than talk and find out who is here again this year.

5.   Give campers free-time options. "You are free
to do what you like until the bell rings. There is
Ping-Pong in the __ , shuffleboard down by the __ ,
crafts in the __ , basketball, ..." Make sure there is
plenty to do. A few may want to help carry
luggage or help in some other way.

You have survived registration. Now get the whole
group together, reintroduce everyone, and move into the
program.

What to Do on the First Day

That first day is critical. Everything that is done sets
a precedent for the week. The first thing the camper will
pick up is your attitude. What will they read?

Will it be:

- "Camp would be more fun without <u>you</u> here."

- "Only one more week and I'll be out of this
place!"

Or will it be:

- "We are going to have a ball TOGETHER this
week!"

- "Can I help you? I really DO care."

The very first hour you will want to communicate the idea to every camper that he is important, accepted, secure, and headed for a wonderful week.

You do this by learning each name quickly, using the camper's correct name (not nickname), listening (and learning!) when they talk, and genuinely caring about each one.

The first meal is important, too. What you allow or expect should be made politely clear. Help the new ones with the camp's routine for entering, serving, cleanup, and leaving. Never correct a camper noisily for doing it wrong. Just show or remind him of the right way. Be positive.

Follow the same procedure for all the camp rules that first day or two. Do not yell or nag, just remind them of the right way and do not allow the wrong way.

In all things, remember that each of your campers came to camp to have a good time — let them.

What to Do When You See Your Cabin Group Has a Wide Cultural Variation

As you greet each camper and help them get settled, listen carefully and observe every one to gain an understanding of what each camper is like.

By the time the last camper checks into your cabin you know that this camp session will be particularly difficult because you have a very wide range of backgrounds: inner city, rural, suburban, Asian, Middle Eastern, African, or a special religious group.

•For younger children, there is so much in common in age group characteristics, that it may not make much difference. You only need to help them learn to accept each other's differences.

•If you work with foreign students, encourage a spirit of — "We want to learn about your country, and we want to enjoy teaching you about ours". This spirit largely depends upon the counselor's own attitudes.

•If you have a mix of "street-smart" kids and culturally refined kids, you have a special problem. It will not be easy but aim for the following:

1. Help them accept each other as being <u>different</u> but <u>not</u> <u>better</u> than each other. Kids do not have a choice about where they grow up.

2. Do not try to mix them. Let each go his own way. Foster a sense of respect for one another's differences and aim for a growing awareness of similarities between the groups.

3. No matter what the background, do not permit that which you know is wrong. This applies to language, actions and attitudes. You will need to establish clear guidelines the very first night.

What to Do on the First Night

The first night <u>can</u> be a problem, but need not be. The night routine that never fails will be discussed fully in another chapter. Let's talk about the particular needs of the first night.

YOUTH CAMP

Sometime during the first day or at night just before story time, go over the rules. (See the chapter 7 on making expectations clear.) The rules you will cover as a cabin will be something like this if you have a grade-school age group:

1. "We are going to have a great time this week, and we are going to do it together."

2. "We don't have a lot of rules, but the ones that we have must be obeyed. Why do you think this is so important?" Let them bring out the reasons for obedience.

3.   "Sometimes another cabin may be doing the wrong thing or be making a lot of noise when they should not, but <u>WE</u> will do what is right."

4.   "We are going to be playing some great new games this week. In most games, someone wins and someone loses. What should we do if we win?" Talk about what it means to be a good sport in winning and in losing.

5.   It's appropriate at this point to give your cabin group a pep talk about being the best cabin. Frame "best" in terms of conduct, honesty, alertness, obedience, cooperation, and so forth. Praise the idea of competition being far above points scored at a game. Measure being the best in terms of character.

TEEN CAMP

In most teen camps, the weekly schedule gives the camper much more freedom. This means that your first night pep talk will take a whole different approach from these five points.

You may want to emphasize cooperation with you as a counselor and the other program leaders, standing up for what is right no matter what others in camp do, or sportsmanship when winning or losing.

Challenge them to be the BEST cabin in these areas as well as in other camp competition.

Here they come, ready or not! Make that first day a <u>GOOD</u> day for every one of your campers.

3 How to Handle Homesickness

There is a word that is never mentioned during camp, at least within earshot of any camper. The very mention of it causes a problem.

If you plan ahead and are ready for it, it need not be a problem at all. Since the word cannot be used, let's call it "it."

For you who are new on the camp scene, the "it" is sometimes spoken right out loud by parents. That's right! In the very presence of the child himself, the parent will even dare to suggest the possibility that their dear little child might become — homesick.

What causes "it"? A child's (or teen's) family is his emotional support. This emotional support is taken for granted until the child finds himself removed from it.

For many, camp is his first experience of separation. When at camp, the child may suddenly sense being stranded, alone. The people he is used to having available are not there. PANIC! "I want to go home! I want my mama!"

The feeling itself is quite real. "It" usually hits in the pit of the stomach and takes over the whole being. However, "it" is primarily a mental/emotional problem and not physical. The real solution lies in solving the real problem.

The problem is a breaking away from traditional emotional support. The solution is growth toward independence and establishing a new emotional support.

This new support system starts when the child comes into camp. Here's what to do...

Make him (or her) feel welcome and never allow him to be lost in the shuffle. Know his name, accept him, show him that you really care.

The day has just ended. It is getting dark. The whole camp family is walking toward their various sleeping quarters. "It" suddenly strikes Karen as she begins to think of her usual night routine at home. Darkness, cabin, trees, sounds, no dog, no mamma — PANIC! PAIN! TEARS! Then you come along side with a firm arm around the shoulder.

"Karen, wasn't that a neat story Uncle Jerry told us in the meeting tonight?"

Her mind is in neutral or stalled out on self. "We aren't finished yet. Lots of girls like the special time we have in the cabin."

Then you go on to dispel her fears by telling her exactly what will happen next. Reassure her of your presence all the time, tell about the funny thing that happened last week, talk about that special day coming up tomorrow.

Above all, keep her moving and thinking about camp.

With children that's all it will take. The sobs might last until sleep comes. You should <u>step</u> <u>over</u> <u>to</u> <u>her</u> <u>bed</u> after "lights-out" and reassure her of your presence and care.

Never mention or talk about home at all.

The next day, at lunch (because Karen is tired and her resistance is down) "it" starts all over again. Normally, just repeat what you did yesterday. Stall for one more day. "Let's get through today and then see how we feel." But let me take it a step further.

Let's assume Karen is something of a problem. She starts to make a scene — will not eat, sobs continually, and insists on calling home and getting picked up today.

What to Do with a Camper
Who Insists on Calling Home

For the camper who has his mind set on calling home and/or going home, there is one basic approach that rarely fails.

You have already been kind and loving, so now you turn into a mild disciplinarian. With firmness that cannot be doubted, you look straight into those bloodshot, teary eyes and overlook the curled lip, and say: "For your benefit, you CANNOT call home and you are not going home. So dry up those tears and get back with your cabin mates. You are staying. Is that clear? Then let's get going." This mild "get tough" approach works MUCH more effectively than piles of sympathy. In fact, using the motherly approach will definitely aggravate the problem.

Cutting off all hope of going back to the home support forces the child to strengthen himself and stand on his feet in a new context.

Another major help is to guide the camper into helping other campers. This takes the focus off himself. There may be a project or some need that he can meet.

Some counselors are quite effective with this type of reasoning: "I've noticed that Jim is new at ping pong. You seem rather good. Would you play with him and help him practice?"

If this problem is mishandled, and the child does go home, it may be difficult for the child to try a sleepover camp again.

If we were to take this problem one step further, we would have a totally different problem. Very few children take the "it" problem to an extreme.

Those who do go to an extreme will not eat right, will not listen in meetings, will insist on their own way, will not try to get over it, and will demand they be allowed to phone home.

If you find yourself with such an obstinate child as this, send him to the Director. He is a discipline problem and needs to be handled as such.

In summary, two things bring on the problem of homesickness. The first we have already discussed — an honest problem you can solve by establishing a new emotional support framework with the individual camper.

The second is the parent. With rare exception the really chronically-ill children were preprogrammed by the parents. Parents will bid the child ado with parting promises, such as "I'm as close as the phone. Just call me if you get "it".

Then there was the parent who wrote about how everyone at home missed him, ..., "and even the cat misses you." If the parent wants to destroy a child this way, there isn't much you can do. But try anyway, for the child's sake.

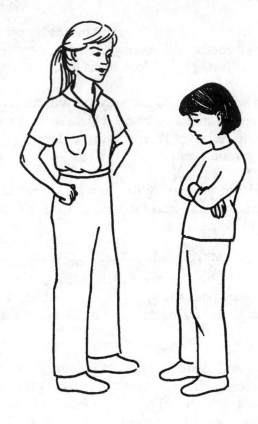

4 How to Make Goals for Campers

During this next week or two at camp, how will the camper GROW in CHARACTER? That answer is largely up to you.

Applying this chapter will make the difference between an average summer and a really great one. If the whole counseling staff will follow these guidelines, the camp itself will rise above the ordinary to the exceptional.

Your first goal is to understand the camper. You can learn a lot by listening with both ears and casually, but intently, observing.

Listen. What is his (or her) vocabulary (i.e., street language, sunday school, educated, slang, polite, crude, etc.)? How does he relate to others in the cabin (i.e., loner, leader, mischief-maker, follower, bully, wallflower)? How does he respond to you, the one who represents authority (i.e., clings, avoids, obeys, disobeys, ignores, pleases, deceives)? Look closely at his eyes, the window to the soul. What do you see (i.e., hurt, loneliness, fear, joy, confidence, life, peace, pride)?

If you can meet his parents, what do you see (i.e., wealth, poverty, confidence, crudeness, character, cigarettes, religious, ...)?

Before the second day of camp is ended, <u>you need to write down a GOAL for every one of your campers</u>. What do you want to make happen in this individual's life this week?

Some Clear Cut Goals

Goals could look something like this:

- That (s)he would overcome shyness and get involved.
- That (s)he would be considerate of other campers.
- That (s)he would learn to be more gentle.
- That (s)he would not be rebellious.
- That (s)he would be content (not complain).
- That (s)he would be more compassionate.

The list can go on and on with character qualities or changes in behavior that you see are needed. The important thing to do is to choose <u>one main objective</u> to see accomplished in that child's life this week.

In choosing an objective, <u>be realistic</u>.

What we CAN expect during the one short week at camp is <u>some</u> change, <u>some</u> movement in the direction of the goal.

After you select a definite goal, <u>write it down.</u> This is essential. Writing it down will force you to make your objective clear, short, and reasonable. At the end of the week (or camping period), write down under the goal the RESULTS. What DID happen in the child's life this week?

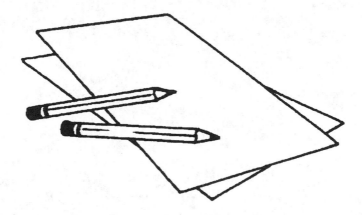

5 How to Be a Successful Counselor

A counselor is one who works with others to solve their personal problems. You may have these children for only one week, perhaps more.

They come to you as total strangers. About Thursday, you feel you are getting to know them rather well, then they leave on Saturday! So what can you do?

Rather than be a counselor in the professional sense of the term, you become an adult friend who understands and still loves. You can help a little toward that camper's understanding of himself and his relationship to others.

Let's see what the camper would appreciate in your "counseling" service to him.

1.	BUILD A RELATIONSHIP. With seven to ten campers in a cabin group, this is not easy. Try to learn their names before they come, and call them by name the first day. Make opportunities to help each one, to talk to each one, to listen to each one.

Avoid the temptation to socialize with your peer group (other staff). Instead, use the snack shop time or free time to get next to a camper.

Play with them in the pool or on the playfield. Take time to teach them a skill: throwing a frisbee, coiling a rope, drawing a picture, or hitting a ball. In these and other ways, invest your life in theirs.

2.   Seek to UNDERSTAND YOUR CAMPERS. Do you know their age group characteristics? Get to know the individual camper by listening and observing carefully.

Remember, all behavior has significance. Every word the child speaks and every action he does will tell you something about him. Casually ask about family, school, pets, friends, and interests, but make careful mental notes on his answers.

3.   SET A GOAL to observe each child at least three times a day. The better you know a child, the more intelligently you can help him.

4.   At least once during the week, MAKE TIME TO TALK to each child personally and privately. Ask them about school, T.V. shows they like to watch, hobbies they may have, sports they like, etc. Your next topic could be related to the goal you have for him or her.

Let's pause here and consider this private talk the counselor will have with each child, because it may be the most significant part of the week.

When to counsel a child is always a problem because the camp schedule is so full.

Eight Specific Times to "Make Friends" with your Camper

Work on using these eight times effectively: free time, snack shop, swim time (by the side of the pool or on the beach), walking to or from the cabin, during cabin cleanup time, when a question is asked, when a child stays back or lags behind, or when there is a fight between two campers.

For example, a fight is a marvelous opportunity to really talk because the camper's "good guy" image is dropped and his real self is exposed. When two campers get in a fight (verbal or otherwise), you have a golden opportunity to take each one aside ALONE and talk to him. The argument itself is only the springboard from which to dive into the real problems and for getting to know your campers.

When questions are asked, are you ready to take advantage of that situation? Above all, BE AVAILABLE, always ready to listen and to take time when it is important to the camper.

BE A GOOD LISTENER. Adults just don't have time for children. Few adults ever really listen to children. Children (and teens) pick this up and read it as a non-caring attitude.

You can make this camper someone super special just by giving him (or her) your undivided attention.

Someone once said that we should relate (that includes listening) to every other person as if he/she were the most important person in the world.

Be aware that listening well has a natural pitfall. It is easy to become emotionally involved in a camper's problems and on the basis of that involvement, begin to take over and give advice. You may find that while you feel good, the camper has been silenced.

Word spreads to the other campers, and they quickly learn to say as little to you as possible. You then assume that everything is going well.

How much better it would have been for you to say nothing until you fully understood what the camper wanted to share with you.

GET TO KNOW each camper. With a full schedule, this is not always that easy. You want to become acquainted with each one and win his confidence. You want to know each one PERSONALLY, as an individual — home background, interests, experiences, church background, etc. You will get to know them by watching all their behavior. Everything they do has significance.

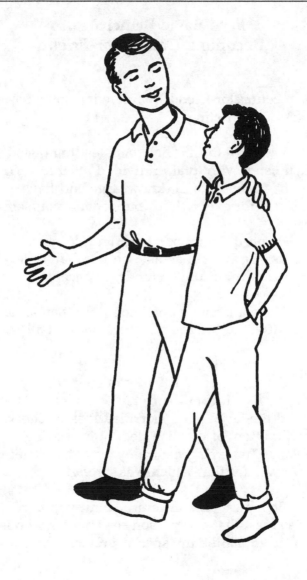

Five Basic Principles to
Become a Counselor-Friend

Be a counselor-friend by following some basic principles of counseling.

1.   Be ready to LISTEN. Ask leading questions and then listen with total undivided attention. You may be the fountain of all knowledge and have all answers for every child, but contain yourself.

2.   Be on the camper's level and do not use big words. Each age has its own vocabulary level and its own level of understanding concepts.

3.   Have a positive attitude rather than an argumentative, or judgmental, or "know-it-all" attitude.

4.   Stay neutral. All that you hear should be received with confidence and calmness. At all costs avoid the facial gasp/horrified look or shock. Beware, too, of devilish delight in hearing sordid details. In staying neutral, you will also not give approval for that which was wrong.

5.   Be honest and sincere. Admit you don't know, or suggest that this person see another who is more skilled to handle the special problem that surfaces.

You need to understand the camper and the situation and then to direct him or her toward the right solution or action. In other words, you are giving advice. Take it easy.

Since you are not in the place of God (all-knowing) you are running a high risk of giving incomplete or even wrong advice.

You also need to help the camper gain insight into herself to understand her own feelings, attitudes, and motives.

We can look at counseling from yet another perspective. Is there a change in behavior that you hope will be accomplished?

If this is the goal, you want that change not to be temporary (only for this one week at camp). This change may need to take place within the person herself: an attitude she holds, guilt that needs resolving, self-acceptance that needs nurturing, etc.

It may be that a change needs to be made in the context of her living: family, school, camp cabin, neighborhood. Do not over-look the possible need for change in the very nature of the person.

Eleven Important Reminders

1.   Counseling takes time. Plan for it. Make it happen.

2.   Keep the confidence of the campers. Something may be humorous to you, but not to him. Take everything seriously, if that is the way it was given to you.

3.   Maintain a cheerful objectivity. Getting emotionally involved will not help at all.

4.   You may want to ask the camper, "What do you think the camp director would do if he were in your place?" This can help him think things through more objectively. Everyone gives advice more easily than he solves his own problems.

5.   Stay within your ability to counsel. Real problems can go into sincere self-image problems, guilt problems, home problems, and more.

6.   Don't get in too deep because far more damage can be done than help given. For the camper's sake, don't let pride take you for a ride at the camper's expense.

7.   Expect patterns of behavior. For example, children often make little problems into big problems. The more you understand the age group

with which you are working, the better counselor you will be.

8.   Remember, not everyone thinks and reacts as you do or as you did when you were a child. In fact, there are five to seven distinctly different ways of handling life situations.

9.   If you run into a counseling problem involving others, work out a solution with those involved after helping to straighten out the attitude of the one with whom you are working.

10.   Encourage independence. Some campers will want to become emotionally dependent upon you and always bring their problems to you. That is very flattering and really helps your ego, but it <u>does not</u> help the camper.

11.   Make sure you follow up on any course of action that you suggest or outline.

20 Specific Questions You Can Ask that Will Help You to Understand Your Campers

To help a child, you need to understand that child. Here are some questions for which you will want to learn answers. You don't get the answers by nailing the kid in a corner and giving him the third degree.

You learn by watching with your eyes and keeping your ears open. Ask the following questions in casual conversation:

- Are your parents at home? Do they work?

- What does your father do? Is he home much? Does he play with you?

- How many brothers and sisters do you have? Where do you fit in?

- How do you get along with your brothers and/or sisters? Do you fight much?

- How many friends do you have? Do you like being alone?

- Do the other kids follow you or do you follow them? Do you get in much trouble?

- What do you like to do? Any hobbies?

- Do you like school? What's your favorite subject? How are your grades?

- What church do you usually attend? How often do you go?

If you wrote a complete description of the camper's actions, what would you include? Go ahead and add to this list, the more you know, the better. Be sure to include qualities that make up the camper's strengths, add to the list throughout the week.

If you seriously desire to understand the camper, you will soon see that taking some kind of notes is imperative. In camp, it is often difficult to keep things confidential, so anything you write down must be carefully guarded. Never leave such a notebook or note cards laying around the cabin!

If you really want to genuinely counsel campers, put a real effort into studying the books by Jay Adams and Dr. James Dobson.

6 How to Handle Problem Children

This Kid Is Driving Me Crazy!

As a counselor, you may experience thoughts like these:

- "Omar is a clown. Everything is a joke with him."

- "Gretchen is a grump. Nothing suits her. I can't figure out why she keeps coming back to camp."

- "Billy is a bully. He's always on one of the smaller guys. He just can't leave them alone."

- "Teresa is terrible. She ALWAYS has to have her own way. The other girls are ready to drown her in the septic tank."

The normal cabin group would have eight to ten campers. Six will be moderately to well behaved. These six will usually do what you ask and earn a 90% on the <u>ideal camper</u> mental check sheet. The other two, three, or four will be in camp so that their parents can get a rest. These four campers make life worth ending.

Three Things You Should Never Do

This normal cabin is usually handled in several wrong ways.

1.   **Never give up control to a camper.** The counselor lets these few run the cabin by giving in to their demands in order to keep the peace. This never works because this small group is self-centered and never satisfied.

2.   **Never spend all of your time on problem kids.** The counselor uses all his time and emotional energy on problem children. This doesn't work because the other "good" children really don't have a counselor this week. They never get his attention, praise, encouragement or help because he is focusing on those that are a problem.

3.   **Never react — you act first.** The few "tough cases" control the counselor by making him stern, aggravated, or even angry. Unfortunately, the whole cabin group must live with these attitudes. The counselor is thus reacting to the few instead of responding to the whole.

If you have an Omar Clown, Billy Bully, Gretchen Grump, or Terrible Teresa, take control of the situation before it takes control of you.

21 Things You Can Do When You Have a Problem Camper (or Two!)

1.   Find out what the problem is. Define it clearly. This is done by your careful listening and observing as well as by asking select and careful questions. (i.e. "Did you do anything to cause your friend to turn against you?" "What do you think started the problem?")

2.   Discover the cause of the problem. Every problem has a cause that is not the problem itself. For example, two campers are fighting. The cause may include a basic selfishness, pride, a spoiled child, a neglectful home, basic thoughtlessness in picking on a weak child, or just immaturity and the old nature in control. If you can't understand the cause, you can't do much to solve the problem.

3.   Show the camper the right solution. It may take some explaining, but he needs to see the right way of handling life's problems. This assumes that you know what is right. You may have to admit you don't have a solution. That's when the camp director or other resource person should be consulted. It is indeed tragic when a counselor has

so much pride that he or she rarely goes for help to those whom the camp has provided.

4.   Take care of the physical needs of each child.

Sleep: Follow the night routine. Insist on a full eight hours or more every night.

Diet: Do not allow the vegetables and fruits to be passed by at meals. Do not allow a heavy diet of candy and sweets. Sugar very often makes junior-age boys wild (hyperactive) and uncontrollable.

Exercise: Some campers avoid it. Encourage plenty of it. The first day, RUN every place you go with them, make it a game.

5.   Take care of the emotional needs of each child.

Self-image: Learn their names, and use their names.

Acceptance: Do not allow one child to pick on another. Encourage total group activity.

Love: Pay special attention to each individual. By attitude and word, leave no doubt in his mind that you really do care.

6.   Encourage self-reliance and accomplishment. Don't do for her what she can do for herself. For little ones, express a "you can do it!" attitude and help him to do it right. Then follow through with praise. For older ones, treat them as adults and compliment them for jobs which are well-done (cabin cleanup jobs, craft projects, etc).

7.   For the child who is ALWAYS doing something wrong, pass over as much as possible, otherwise his camp experience will be like home and school — overseen by dissatisfied and rejecting adult authority figures. In private counseling, help her to see her self-defeating cycle of behavior, and help her to choose alternative responses to problems.

8.   Always be looking for an opportunity to praise and compliment. Even the seemingly proud and boastful child sees himself as worthless and unworthy.

9.   Be extremely fair when giving out any form of discipline: a word of correction, a cross look, a penalty, anything. The problem child is always being blamed, but I have found that such a child is often "set up" by another more crafty child (or

teen). The crafty one hangs back and privately smirks as the "victim" gets into trouble. Be careful. Never assume a child is guilty of an offense.

10.　　Give directions, rules, or expectations very clearly. Children, especially those who misbehave, often do not hear or do not understand what is really expected. Some disobedience is actually a hearing or attention problem.

11.　　When children sharply disagree, they often try to settle it with a physical fight. "Might makes right" is their false value system. A frustrated counselor may want to sink to that level, too. Don't.

If you find yourself using physical force to make a child obey or to discipline him, <u>you are wrong</u>.

Yes, there are rare exceptions, but you are safer following basic principles. Keep your battle on the level of will power, then you can always win while maintaining respect. You may win by using physical force, but you lose the respect of the cabin group, and a dangerous precedent is set.

12.　　Be WITH a child, never AGAINST him. Make a conscious effort to surround and approach every problem or problem child in such a way as to be clearly on his side.

For example, you might say to Billy Bully in a low and confidential tone: "Billy, you're a strong guy, and the other guys would like to have you as a friend, but you have to treat them right. By shoving them around and always trying to get your own way, you are causing the guys to turn against you. I don't want that to happen. What do you think you could do to earn their respect and friendship?" You are with him and on his side, but not approving his behavior.

13.   De-emphasize winning and re-emphasize each success. A problem child is often the loser, so play down the camp contests. At the same time, notice good table manners (if you can find them!), a bed made well, cooperation given, effort put forth, or whatever positive thing you can find.

14.   In private counseling, help him see the results of his actions. Gently, but firmly, make him take full responsibility for his actions and their results. Suggest or ask him for alternative ways to behave and react.

15.   Separate the child from the group. Because of high sugar intake, emotional disturbance, a super giddy mood, home problems, lack of sleep, body chemical imbalance, or boredom, the camper may be giving you a very low level of cooperation and thus be destroying the spiritual emphasis of the hour.

Rather than reacting in anger, simply separate him. In chapel, put him in the aisle seat and <u>you</u> sit next to him. In class put him in the extra chair in the back of the room. In the dining hall, have him sit alone at the other end until the dishes are cleared. In the cabin after lights out, put him outside for 15 minutes (see the night routine for details on this).

In any case, help him to understand <u>why</u> you are separating him — that you cannot allow him to destroy this special time for others.

16.   Help the child AVOID being disciplined by guiding him away from conflicts and problems. Keep him away from that other camper who always causes a conflict. Seat him on the end of the row. Put his bunk near yours. Assure his success as much as possible. "Head him off at the pass" if he is going toward trouble. Work <u>with</u> him in this, and you will be his friend.

17.   Always BE THERE! Most problems between campers arise because the counselor was not there. Lack of supervision is a major cause of accidents, too. BE where the campers are. This one principle will solve many, many problems.

18.   Exemplify love. It's tough to fight against someone who loves you.

19.   Ridicule, sarcasm, and negative jesting are evils that will destroy your relationship and destroy the child's self-image. Even though your frustration factor is running high, don't use these weapons. Don't ever use these weapons!

20.   When problems do arise, never take ONE side of a story. Always seek to learn the whole truth from each person involved and through witnesses. Quiet children may require a private talk to get them to tell the truth due to fear of others or peer pressure. You must know the truth before you can work on the real problem.

21.   Seize the chance to counsel. A camper that's "driving you crazy" is a camper who is giving you multiple opportunities to counsel with her. In that private counseling situation, your first objective is to help the camper take responsibility for her own actions.

As you talk to these children, the common denominator is irresponsibility. They blame their actions and attitudes on their parents, the camp, the counselor, the other campers, or even society, but they themselves take no responsibility.

Your counseling should take this path: take responsibility, admit guilt, ask forgiveness, make it right with others. There is no growth in character without this path being taken.

This brings us naturally to the next problem, discipline of campers who misbehave. Before we jump into that often neglected topic, let's back up to "an ounce of prevention is worth a pound of cure."

7

How to
Prevent Trouble

Young people do not come to camp to be bawled out, yelled at, denied privileges, scolded, harassed, threatened, scared, and tortured. They don't come to be the pawns of a power hungry counselor. <u>They come to have a good time!</u>

It's your job to ensure that this objective is achieved, as well as the camp's objective.

You must keep the spirit of the cabin very positive, with cooperation, excitement, anticipation, mutual respect, orderliness, and contentment in order to reach these objectives.

Take Nothing for Granted

The ideal cabin is created the very first day of the camping session. Some of your children have been coming here for years, but each counselor was different. Some campers have been to Camp WaHoo, where anything goes. Others have never been to camp before.

On the first day, weld this group together. How? Give them a grand pep talk! Emphasize ours being the <u>BEST</u> cabin this week, the NEATEST, the hardest working, the sharpest etc. Then spell out exactly what is expected.

<u>Never assume the campers know what is expected.</u>

Go over the rules of the camp, the rules of the cabin, the expectations of obedience and cooperation, and who is in charge.

If you are laying down the rules, try to do it with some humor, and come around <u>with</u> them. Keep reminding them; they tend to forget easily.

Show how all of this will help them to have a good time.

Make the expectations quite clear: "When I am talking, you are not talking. When someone is talking to the whole camp family, all of us listen. When it's time to sing, everyone sings; even if you croak like a frog, croak loudly. Maybe there will be another frog in tune with you! Boys, stay out of the girls' cabin area at all times, no exceptions. (Same goes for the girls.) When the bell rings, THIS cabin will be there first and look the sharpest. Right?"

When you give the pep talk and lay down the rules, try to make every rule clear for their own benefit. As their leader, you are 100% WITH them and for them. Keep your rules to a minimum, too.

Again, remember why they came to camp. There is no need to make a new rule every time there is a new problem; just work with the problem. A few basic principles can cover a lot of territory: be kind one to another; no physical contact; obey those in authority.

Here are the basic rules for the counselor who must make rules:

1. Make the expectations or rules known from the very beginning of camp.

2. Make them clear.

3. Make each one for the group's benefit.

4. Give them with humor and kindness.

5. Make as few as possible.

Four Ways to Get
Respect from Your Camper

1.   Make your expectations clear.

2.   Earn their respect.

   Respect isn't earned by being physically big, by yelling, by having a title, or by lording it over others.

Respect is earned by reputation, by assumption, by conduct, and by maintaining the gap. Your reputation is what the campers <u>think</u> you are.

Word spreads quickly between campers: "Mr. Joe is a great guy, and he means what he says." "Polly is a pushover. You can get away with most anything." "Mr. Steve is never around. He's in love with Tilly, the life-guard."

Respect is earned by reputation. Be consistent from day to day.

3.   Respect is earned by assumption. You must ASSUME your role as the authority figure and leader and thus tactfully demand respect that is appropriate for your position.

Many times you can observe a camper who quickly becomes the peer group leader. Watch closely and you will see that this child simply ASSUMES the authority to tell the others what to do, and they do it! Take command, and <u>they will follow</u>.

Respect is earned and maintained by your conduct. Are you deserving of their respect? Your conduct and general manners must be above reproach.

A camper will not respect a counselor who picks on the fat kid, assumes George is always guilty, leaves the cabin unattended, does a sloppy job in giving lessons, uses sarcasm and ridicule, or spends more time with his girl friend than his cabin of boys. Even a child will not respect the 250-pound Mr. Macho who behaves like this.

Respect assumes a looking up to another person. This means you must maintain the gap between them by being a leader and not a camper. There are already nine, nine-year olds in the cabin; they don't need or want a tenth who is chronologically over twenty. Being too much one of them is a sad but repeated mistake made by many counselors.

4.   Remember this, <u>you'll never earn their respect if you don't also respect them!</u> That's right. You must respect little seven-year old Dirty Face Danny.

Your respect is evidenced in the words you choose (no sarcasm), in your tone of voice (how would you address the guest speaker at a conference?), and in the way you give directions.

Do you order them around like a sergeant, or preface your request with "please" and follow through with a "thank you." Do you know their names? Do you? When they have a problem that is real to them, let it be real to you, too. Take them seriously.

How to Maintain Control

Discipline problems can be prevented by an early and clear understanding of expectations, by earning respect, by giving respect, and by maintaining control.

Someone <u>will</u> be in control, either you or a camper. Control will greatly reduce the need to discipline, as well as maintain a good spirit.

Maintaining control is not as hard as you think. Put away the six-shooter and bull whip. They are not needed. Just BE where the action is.

If your campers are in the cabin, you are. If they are at the pool, so are you. Wherever they are, you are. Simple? Yes. Standard procedure for most counselors? No. Give it all you have.

Take your role as leader seriously, and your campers will take you seriously. Then when you speak, they will listen.

When a 200-pound sailor boy in full uniform walked into my cabin as a camper, I had to make a quick decision; "Who is in charge?" I treated him just like the rest, assumed my role as the leader, and had the whole cabin with me.

To maintain control, always be one step ahead of the group. When they plan that unofficial night visit to the girls' cabin, you are ready with a flashlight and a fake sleep routine. When their hand reaches for the door, suddenly the spot light goes on. "Surprise!" You are in control.

8

How to
Discipline in Camp

Discipline does not mean clobbering kids, making life miserable, or playing army sergeant. It does mean maintaining individual and group cooperation so that camp goals are accomplished.

Prevention is always easier than cure. In addition to those measures mentioned in chapter 7, add these: a basic attitude of humility, care in showing no favoritism, doing things with the camper, fairness in all decisions, a good sense of humor, a desire to serve the campers (instead of being the big boss), not seeking applause or appreciation, a heart's desire to minister to needs, and an attitude of love for every camper.

If you follow through and use these preventive measures, will all discipline problems dissolve? Most books assume that you will not have problems. Ninety percent of the time this is true. Now about that ten percent.

When Selfish Sally or Lazy Larry need to be brought back into line, the first step is to remind yourself and to explain to them exactly why you cannot allow misbehavior.

Four Reasons Why
We Must Have Discipline

1.   Discipline is always <u>for</u> the camper. He is missing out on part of the fun and the heart beat of camp by not being "in" with the others.

     His behavior is causing him to lose friends. If he is not corrected, he will be learning something which is wrong, and we can't allow that. He also needs training in self-control and subordination.

2.   Discipline is for the camp. One person can't be allowed to spoil things for everybody else. No one has the right to be destructive in any form (destroying property, spirit, attitudes, etc.).

     Please note the attitude with which we approach the camper. We are FOR her and we are coming alongside her. You must make sure that she knows that we are not against her or she won't respond appropriately. Then the discipline will be ineffective.

3.   Discipline is maintained for the sake of the other campers. They have a right to security, safety, food, rest, a good time, and spiritual help. No one camper has the freedom to deny these things to others.

4.   Discipline is for the counselor. You need to maintain your leadership role and your position. However, never take revenge for something done to you, personally. Let another one in authority deal with such a problem.

We are back to the 10% who have the most wonderful counselor in the world (you!) and still cause a problem. What can you do?

First ask yourself <u>why</u> he is behaving that way. If possible, remove the temptation, situation, or surroundings that cause the misconduct. Then help him back on his feet and back onto the right track. Talk with him.

Six Commonly Used Methods and Which Ones Work

1.   Do the easiest thing first. Quite often, all that is needed is for you to <u>say something</u>. Most problems could be avoided if the one in authority stopped the misconduct with just a word when he saw it developing. "John, that's enough. Stop, please," will usually end the problem.

2.   Another method used is the "Big Stick" method. Basically this method says: "I'm bigger than you, so you had better do what I say." This does work,

temporarily, but it often creates bigger problems of rebellion, disrespect, and antagonism.

Young, athletic, male counselors have often used this method. It <u>seems</u> to work because they see the boys responding. The positive response may be an initial admiration of Mr. Big Guy, but when the Big Guy isn't around, there is little respect.

So, even if you get good results, don't do what you know is wrong just because it works for a while.

3.   A third method, used by frustrated and immature counselors, is threat. If you put the use of threats in the context of all else that has been taught herein, little room is left for them.

If you do make threats, keep these basic rules: (1) Always be prepared to carry them out, or else the camper will call your bluff. (2) Never threaten with cruel or radical punishment. "Either shut up or I'll stick your head in a toilet!" Is that right? (3) Never threaten beyond your power to enforce. The counselor does not have power to send a child home, spank, or deny meals. So when do you use threats? Perhaps a few examples would help clarify the principles.

Rest time with free swimming or store time next:

"We have exactly 50 minutes left (with pencil in hand). When you guys are lying flat on your bed and quiet, your 50 minutes starts. If anyone keeps on messing around, he and I will stay and take our rest hour while the others go swimming." (You have thus made it a game, a challenge, and a threat. Be prepared to stay late!)

Meal time and one camper will not settle down or obey:

"Jody, you will either have to settle down and eat, or you will sit in the back corner of the dining hall until we have finished." (Be ready with a chair. Save the meal and let him eat when everyone has gone. Use this as a last resort.)

In a meeting or at a campfire council, two children will not stop talking to each other or making a disturbance:

Either move over and sit between them or lean over to whisper to them. "You guys pay attention to Mr. Righttruth or you can have a special seat in the back with Mr. Firmhand" (Yes, <u>DO</u> move them during the meeting if they continue. No third and fourth and fifth warnings, please!)

On the playfield, Proud Pat is giving the others a hard time when they miss the ball. You call him to one side and tell him:

"Either you stop criticizing and cutting down the other players or you can sit with Miss Lovenoball on the sidelines." Later on, when he is sitting on the sidelines, use this as a counseling opportunity.

4.   One of the most effective tools is the "counselor with camper talk." You talk to the camper as one person to another. This assumes your respect and assumes he (or she) is going to carry responsibility.

Discuss the reasons for the conduct and the natural consequences. The key to success is your approach and your mental attitude. You are working out a problem as an employer would do with an employee whom he trusted and respected.

Example: Sue Slop is the one who makes her cabin lose points because her bed isn't neat, and her things are not in order. You pick a time when it is just you and she, alone.

"Sue, the other girls really want to get honor cabin tomorrow. What do you think

you can do to help?" No doubt the others
have made it quite clear that Sue Slop is
ruining their cabin record.

"Let's tackle this problem together. How can I
help you have the neatest bed in the cabin?" Make
it clear that you are WITH her, and not against her.
You also need to really teach her how to do some
things, too. Make it a fun project that you do
together.

5.   This method requires a lot of common sense.
Children are children, and they act like it. Much of
their so-called misbehavior is only childishness.
Rather than calling them on every move, just ignore
their behavior.

In every camp the counselors very soon find the
one or more children who are ALWAYS doing
something wrong. It seems they cannot even
breathe right (it's into someone's face or "down
your neck").

If you were to correct this child, that is ALL you
would do all day, every day. For that child, establish basic and minimal boundaries and correct him
every time these lines are crossed. You might call
him aside after one day (the first evening) and
explain.

"This is a fine camp. We do things differently. We do not swear or tell dirty jokes. Fighting isn't a solution we use. We do not hit others. There's only one king of the castle (the counselor)." It is imperative that you NOT scold him or verbally walk all over him. You are WITH him and want him "to have the best possible week, and this is the way to do it."

6.   This method is particularly good for the very young campers but will also work occasionally with older ones. I call it "Diversion into fun." Let's consider the older campers first.

One cause of disciplinary problems with older campers is too much free time. The solution is to have a camp program that is positively FULL of things to do. If you see trouble brewing, divert the group or individual into something fun to do.

- "Hey, the snack shop is opening in 10 minutes; let's beat the other cabin there."

- "I'll give my dessert at supper to the first one to the dining hall. Go!"

- "Let's challenge the Omaha cabin to a game of soccer."

- "Have you guys hiked to the maple grove yet? We have an hour, let's go."

For the younger campers, this method can often be used and used often on a smaller scale.

- "Billy, would you play frisbee with Hank?"

- "George, help me put this cabin back in order, would you?"

- "I'll challenge the winner at tetherball!"

- "Sally and Liz get the fire going. Mary, lay out the food. Julie, get more water. And the rest of us will scout up wood."

- "Would you find Uncle Heartful and invite him to eat with us tonight?"

If discipline in the form of punishment needs to be used, whether it's just a word spoken or cooling off time in the corner of the dining hall, there are basic principles of discipline that need to be followed.

Three Forms of
Discipline <u>Never</u> to Use

Several forms of "discipline" are NEVER to be used. These forms come from the counselor's frustration, anger, immaturity, or plain cruelty.

1.   Never use ridicule, shaming or sarcasm. These things are a direct attack upon the camper himself rather than the action of the camper.

This gruesome threesome will help destroy the camper's self-image, may set negative examples for the camper to use towards others, will not change the behavior pattern, and certainly will be a negative influence on the counselor-camper relationship.

Sarcasm is so common between staff members that it's quite "normal" to apply it to campers. Sarcasm does not measure up to high standards of conversation. It is not kind, does not edify, and is not "seasoned with salt" as our conversation should be. ALL sarcasm has to go. Sarcasm, even among staff, builds a negative atmosphere.

2.   Never use cruelty. A few counselors get so-called bright ideas as to how to make kids behave. They make them sit under an outside light at night in their underwear and let them get eaten alive by bugs. They pick them up by their heels and stick their heads in a toilet.

Each camp has its own set of cruel and unusual punishments for campers. But is outright cruelty and fear the right way to care for children? Of course not!

3.   Never strike a camper. These same immature counselors sometimes resort to hitting campers. It's the old "I'm bigger than you are, so shape up" philosophy.

As campers negatively react to a poor counselor the counselor is often the target of that reaction. How wrong it is for a good counselor to respond in kind with **vindictive punishment.**

An easy-way-out kind of discipline is **deprivation.** The scenario usually goes something like this: "If you don't stop messing around you can't go to swimming this afternoon!"

Deprivation means the counselor takes some normal camp activity away because the camper misbehaved. The child came to camp to have a good time, and now the counselor threatens to take away what the child came to get! This may be an entire meal, a dessert, store time, swim time, game time, or any other positive fun time.

Deprivation should be primarily the choice of the camp director over the counselor. It should, in any case, be used only sparingly and carefully.

Back to Basics — Six Principles

1.   Discipline should follow the offense as soon as possible. In a child's thinking, there is no connection (i.e.,no response or change of behavior) between settling down to sleep on Tuesday night and losing swimming privileges on Wednesday afternoon.

      Do something IMMEDIATELY if disciplinary action is needed. Do the easiest first: say something ("Frank, don't swing on the rafters; come on down.") If a child is talking during chapel, stretch your arm and tap him on the shoulder, or move over to sit next to him.

      Do it NOW, rather than bawl him out later and take privileges away.

      Suppose a camper is misbehaving at the table after being spoken to several times. In the middle of his horseplay, take him away from the table to a lonely chair somewhere else. Don't wait until later to do something because he will not remember what he has done or what his actions caused.

      The camper must get a mental and emotional connection between the misdeed and the consequences. A time lag can erase that connection.

2.   Relate the misdeed to the punishment. If she
            disobeys the swimming rules, she sits on the ground
            by the lifeguard for 15 minutes.

            If she doesn't eat the main part of the meal, she
            doesn't eat the dessert either.

            If she wastes materials in the craft shop, she is
            charged for them or is limited in what she is
            allowed to do.

            If she makes continued disturbances in class, she
            is put in the back of the room next to a leader.

            If she does not follow the safety rules at riflery,
            she is put on the sidelines for the period.

            In all of these examples, there is no time lag and
            the punishment was appropriate for the misconduct.

3.   Was the conduct WILLFUL or just CARELESS?
            If there is a doubt, give the benefit of the doubt to
            the camper. Many things children (and teens) do is
            just childish carelessness. Such actions may be
            worthy of words of caution, but they do not merit
            actual punishment or deprivation of any kind.

            At the table children spill things and make a
            mess; take time to teach table manners. At night in
            the cabin, they don't know what to do next in the
            night routine; guide them in getting organized.

In potentially dangerous camp activities (swimming, archery, riflery, canoeing) they do foolish things in order to copy something they saw on T.V. Teach them basic safety and procedures BEFORE they can even touch the equipment.

Prevent and forgive carelessness; respond appropriately to willful disobedience.

4.   Punish to the point of regret. The purpose for punishment is to make the conduct an unpleasant experience so the camper will not want to repeat it.

You want to get the message across so that it doesn't pay to misbehave. Whether or not you can actually accomplish this depends on the camper.

If a tough nut has adopted the pattern of behavior that frequently breaks rules, the best you can do with any punishment is to make the misbehavior not totally rewarding and clearly not acceptable.

Above all, be fair. Do not overdo the punishment. Your purpose is to give EVERY camper a great week at camp. You are NOT running a reformatory.

5.   After a disciplinary action, try to talk with the camper. He needs to know that you really do care

and that your actions are for him and not against him.

Quite often during or at the end of a disciplinary action (seated on the sidelines, taken out of the action, sent to the director) there is a great opportunity to lovingly counsel the camper.

Usually the camper experiences adult temper, frustration, or even abuse when he misbehaves. Now, in your camp, he gets only fairness, love, concern, and counsel. What a contrast!

Often, after a child is disciplined at home (i.e.,yelled at and sent to his room), the punishment is seen as a result of the adult's anger, <u>NOT</u> as a result of his own behavior.

If you will follow these guidelines and basic principles, you can counsel the child into taking responsibility for his actions.

Taking responsibility is the FIRST step toward real change in behavior.   Every person must accept full responsibility for his (or her) own actions.

6.   Administration of discipline is teamwork. The "Who" of discipline can be crucial to its effectiveness. You are the primary administrator, but there should be others that can help when needed.

In most of the examples given, you're the one who must administer discipline quickly, in relation to the offense, fairly, and with pure motives. But there are times when you must put aside your pride and humbly use other team members. (See page 70)

What to do with a Bully

A bully may be a boy or girl, the biggest or the smallest. His one outstanding characteristic is that he deliberately and consistently pulverizes some other camper, usually when the counselor is out of sight. He may choose one victim or he may try to terrorize the whole cabin. He may actually attempt giving internal ruptures, or he may be all mouth and threats.

As the counselor, keep in mind the following:

- Be careful not to be "against" this camper, but be the protector of the ones he/she is abusing. The bully needs to get this message loudly and clearly from the counselor.

- Never leave this camper alone or out of sight. Alert other staff to help you.

- Once you have ONE clear case of abuse by this camper to another, take him aside privately and explain the camp rules and the consequences of his/her actions.

- Give him a 24 hour test period restriction. For example, for the next 24 hours he cannot leave the counselor's sight without permission. If he gives the counselor or any other camper a hard time, he will have a long visit with the camp director.

What to Do When
You're Abused by a Camper

When a camper abuses you with fighting or name calling, always arrange for someone else to handle the problem. If you correct the child, it looks to him like self-defense.

However, as you teach respect for authority, always work <u>with</u> the camper, not against him/her.

If it is a minor incident (disrespectfully addressing the counselor, inappropriate jesting, ...), the junior counselor should step in and speak to the camper and reset appropriate standards.

If further action needs to be taken, or if the situation is more serious, the next higher one in the camp organizational structure should speak to the camper as soon as possible. This may be the Head Counselor, Program Director or Director.

Your pride is the primary obstacle in the team approach to discipline. Pride says, "I can handle it. I do not need help."

Learn from My Mistake

I'll never forget sending a camper to the Camp Director. It was a teen snow camp in upper Wisconsin. This camper had a good supply of fire crackers. Repeatedly, he had been dropping them one at a time into the cabin's wood stove. I told him how dangerous it was, but he only waited for me to turn my back for a moment. This guy was incorrigible.

I lost my temper and marched him up to the Camp Director, a dear old grandfather-type I fully expected a royal bawling out for this camper and a few choice threats.

I was crushed. The director just sat this guy down and talked to him as a loving father, kind, gentle, and understanding. Of all the nerve! At the end of the week the campers filled out forms that included evaluation of the counselor. I lost the respect of the good kids when I lost my temper at the bad ones. I should have called for help sooner.

I learned four things:

1.   The higher authority does not and should not adopt the frustration of the lower authority. The higher the authority, the more we need to see mature qualities in evidence.

2.   The lower authority needs to utilize the mature wisdom of the higher authority. Humility will enable him (or her) to recognize when he may be at the end of his rope and not know how to effectively deal with a problem.

3.   Teamwork in discipline needs to be used BEFORE the counselor messes things up.

4.   The camp leadership needs to back up counselors and not leave them stranded. The leadership needs to work closely with the counselors, know what is happening, and be a team that works together. In too many camps the counselor is on his (or her) own. This is a tragic mistake.

Teamwork

Teamwork can work for you and make camp doubly effective. When there is a problem camper (a camper who has a problem!), other staff can help, too. Yes, the kitchen workers, the craft assistant, and the maintenance workers, too. Enlist their help. Ask them to:

1.   Be polite to him (or her), even though the camper may be "asking for a nose job." Do not react, but respond. Give him what he needs, not what he deserves.

2.   Learn his (or her) name and call him (or her) by name. Use his name! It shows real interest and respect. However tempting, do not use nicknames. Usually such names only increase the problem. I remember a fat little kid we dubbed "Butterfly Boy" because he seemed to always be chasing butterflies with his net. What he needed was genuine caring, not mocking.

3.   Do not talk about her to others. Usually such conversation degenerates into non-complimentary "evaluations" that have a way of getting back to the camper. Once the camper loses respect for the staff through this, she will not be cooperative with the camp. Is it worth the risk?

4.   Find time or excuses to talk to him: snack shop time, free swim period, before meals, when waiting in line, etc. The more that people talk to him as a person, the more we are working on some of the real problems such as low esteem.

9 How to Put a Camper to Bed

At Camp WaHoo the kids have a blast! The first night is spent in riotous living. "Lights out" occurs three or four times the first night, and finally the counselor goes to sleep so the campers don't have to listen to his, "Now this is the last time I'm going to tell you ...." About 3:00 a.m. the last camper sleeps from exhaustion.

The last night of camp has more order to it. The boys have planned a special party — without the counselor, of course, but including the girls.

The counselor rejoices at the grand cooperation and falls to sleep quickly. Then the fun really begins. When the staff members are coming back from THEIR party, they wake up the counselor and tell him that his kids are down at the lake with the girls.

In order to gain the most from his/her experience at camp, each camper needs to be mentally awake and emotionally stable. If you want cooperation, participation and fewer problems, getting a full night's sleep is absolutely essential to the accomplishing of these goals.

"Kids love darkness rather than light because the counselor can't see."

There is plenty of fun during the day, and perhaps a few well-orchestrated evening or night activities. Putting the camper to bed ON TIME and giving him (requiring?) a full night's sleep will not detract at all from the program of the camp, but it will help greatly.

You can do it without yelling and threatening. Actually, it can be a lot of fun. Anyone can do it. The following method has been very successfully used for years with young people from the ages of 7 to 18.

Step 1: To the Cabin

The evening activity or campfire has just ended. You're heading back to the cabin, which means BED for the campers. The game begins. "What can we do to avoid ending today?" is their goal. Your counter move is simply to WALK WITH THEM. Sound easy? Sure is! Unless you have a "special" friend who is counselor in the other half of camp. Campers first! Walk with them. Here's why.

1.   This avoids the need to scold later because they got "lost" going to the cabin.

2.   This gives another special opportunity to get to know them and their reactions to the meeting.

3.   You easily keep them moving in the right direction by moving in that direction yourself.

4.   It is a constructive way to give that personal attention and show real interest in individuals. You are establishing better rapport.

The only side trip for campers at this point may be to the nurse. Older ones can be sent. Younger ones may need to be taken or sent with a more responsible camper. Note: Do this NOW or else you will have a major interruption during lights out or even later.

Step 2: How to
Handle the First Big Stall

You all made it to the cabin. Congratulations! Now, remind them of the next step. "Everyone get your toothbrush. We want to get to the wash-house before everyone else gets there!" Make it a game or contest if you can.

Now comes the first BIG STALL. Remember, the objective for the camper is to avoid at all costs that inevitable "lights out" time. He feels it coming closer, so he may try several maneuvers.

- "Who took my toothbrush! I left it right here!" Or the towel isn't around (it's on the line where he left it).

- He may just stand there, talk, and goof around with his buddy.

- As they fly out the cabin door, one may detour to the cabin next door.

- When finally AT the wash-house, rather than really washing up, the little water fight starts or a "deep discussion" on how the other team cheated (our team lost).

These are children (even if teens), so this behavior is normal. To counteract it, just patiently remind each one, ONE AT A TIME, what he OUGHT to be doing; then (now get this technique) just stand there and watch him until he does it. Simple, effective, and kind.

Please note that the counselor is WITH the campers the whole time. There is an art to getting through the night routine yourself AND getting your campers through it. If you are working with a junior counselor, plan how to alternate the responsibility so both of you can be ready for the next step.

Step 3: Back to the Cabin

Getting some cabin groups through the wash-up routine is like trying to hold onto eight slippery fish. Don't give up, be patient.

The FIRST thing to do when a camper gets back to the cabin is to ask, "Did you go to the toilet?" Phrase it how you like, but make sure it is clearly understood. The rule is, EVERYBODY GOES. No excuses.

Step 4: How to Handle the Second Big Stall

The camper will not give a straight answer to your question because (s)he knows that "I have to go" is an excuse that never fails during cabin lights out, or later. Listen carefully for a straight and truthful response.

"I don't have to go." "I went after supper." Answer with a big smile or humor, but make it stick. "Try again, EVERYBODY goes."

At this point each one should be changing into his/her P.J.'s but some may be slow to the extreme. The basic rule is that NO CLOTHES are worn to bed that have been worn all day. For those not changing, try this: "O.K., Joe, let's start with the shoes. Now the socks. Now keep going until you are in bed."

You stand there a few seconds and just watch until he really starts. If this does not work, go to the next step. "You either do it yourself or I'll have to do it for you."

This is said with a big smile, of course. But stick with it! The farthest I've ever had to go was the shoes.

We need to pause here and make a special note. Some children are just embarrassed to change in front of others. So clue them in on how to do it under the covers quickly and quietly, rather than force them or ridicule them.

I've often told little guys, "Do it quickly now, everyone is changing and no one will notice." "Get back to the cabin early tomorrow night and be done by the time most get here." In any case, work WITH the camper, and he will appreciate it.

Step 5: Into Bed!

Most are changed into night clothes. The bathroom visits have ceased. But as you look around the cabin, no one is in bed.

Give them a time limit or a goal. "O.K., in just 60 seconds I want everyone IN BED and ready to go to sleep, but we'll have story time first before lights out." Most will enjoy the contest.

With older ones, you may need a few gentle but firm reminders: "Sam, let's get going. Don't hold up the cabin."

Help individuals (especially those that are slightly scatter-brained or disorganized) to quickly take care of last minute details and hop into bed. Work WITH them to meet the deadline and keep the countdown coming.

Once you get a camper into bed, don't let him get out!

Step 6: Story Time

We are speaking here of how to get campers into bed and asleep on time, so the discussion of how to conduct an evening cabin story time will be taken up later.

Start the story even with a little noise in the cabin. Start with a question, or something else.

Step 7: The "Last Word"

Just before you begin, or perhaps you will want to stop in the middle, give this little speech: "I'm going to read a short story (or poem). When I say "the end" that's it for the night — no more talking or questions or bathroom visits."

At the end of the story time or discussion, be standing near the light switch. If you are reading the story, as you read the last paragraph, flip off the light switch and finish with a flash light.

Remember, they are all in their beds and ready to go to sleep (you hope!). So you say, "The End."

"O.K. guys, this is our last ditch effort to stall off going to bed!" is the thought in several young, creative minds. Counselor, are you ready for —

Step 8: How to
Handle the Third Big Stall

1. "I have to go to the bathroom!" "Me too!" Did he go before? Did you, as counselor, make SURE he went? Then you have one pat answer: "No." Of course, if you forgot to ask him, he has you. You lose, and he wins.

    If that is the case, send them ONE at a time. If you DID check one at a time and he said he DID go, then you tell him, "No, you will have to wait till morning." He says, "But I gotta go" and breaks the whole cabin up with laughter.

    At this point I pull out my old standard reply that has become a standing joke in my camps: "Sorry, no deal. Medical records prove that you can wait 12 hours without any physical harm. If there is a mess in the morning YOU can clean it up."

In short, hold your ground!

2.   Following this go-round or instead of it, there are all kinds of "important" comments to cabin mates or wise cracks. Some even try the old "Good night Sam, Good night Ollie, ..." and go around the cabin. Then the next one picks it up and does the same.

3.   Of course, now the campers get very respectful and want to ask you, the father of all wisdom, some important questions.

Girls often appear to get very serious at this point.

For all these important questions and comments, you have only one stock answer: "I said that's it for today, no more talking tonight." "I'll answer that tomorrow, not tonight. Good night." or "Sh-sh-sh, no more tonight, tomorrow's another day."

Remember, once you answer a question, you have broken your own rule about talking, so, MANY other questions will follow. YOU said "no more talking"; therefore, the most basic principle is this: YOU cannot continue a conversation either.

Beware of this trap. MOST COUNSELORS fall for this one and the kids know it.

The second basic principle is not obvious: Always speak quietly to the individual who is talking, NOT to the group.

Say as little as possible yourself, say it softly, and say it only to ONE person. Never again, the rest of the night, will you address the cabin as a whole. ALWAYS speak only to the one person.

"Why?" The mental game they play is this: "She is really speaking to the others, so I am getting away with it." You crash their game when you address him by name: "Lucy, no more. We are done."

If you have 5 talking, go to each one's bed and give him the same message with just a little variation. "No matter what the others do, YOU quit. No more."

The third principle is this: you must stay on your feet in the middle of the cabin. If you were sitting on your bed when you said "The End," stand up in the middle of the dark cabin immediately. Just stand there.

For each disturbance, go to that person's bunk and speak to him. Being on your feet will help you get quickly and quietly to where the problem is. An added benefit is that the whole cabin will be quiet to hear what you are telling Lucy in her ear!

Stay in the cabin; do not leave. If you leave now for that staff party (or special "friend"), the alert camper will assume leadership and start his own party.

In any case, every camper must ALWAYS have some responsible adult there. It is a basic of good child care. Never leave campers alone. NEVER.

"Our Last Chance"

So you won the first round, but these campers are not about to give up! "O.K., so he's got us on the talking routine, but let's try another angle."

Step 9: How to Handle the Fourth Big Stall (THE BIG JOKE)

Usually it comes after story time and often after the talking has stopped. The little geniuses will start with the mouth noises, rubbing or bumping the wall, crinkling paper, throwing little objects to a friend, playing with a flashlight, or the methodic rolling back and forth in the squeaky old army bed.

Hang in there, counselor, you WILL win the game!

1.   Stay on your feet in the middle of the cabin. When you know who is doing it, go to that ONE

person and tell him to stop (the action) because it's time to go to sleep, not play games. Part of the game he is playing is, "Does the counselor know what I'm doing?" You won the game!

2.   If you need to calm a camper down, speak ever so softly close to him and give him a lecture that would put anyone to sleep! Tell him he's been a good camper; it's been a good day; let's end the day right; much to do tomorrow so we need a full night's sleep; it is not right to keep the others awake, etc., etc., etc.

When You Go to Bed

IF you will use this method, you will find that you will be getting much more sleep. In fact, all you want.

You are on your feet in the middle of a dark cabin. Several campers have had the pleasure of your personal visit. The games seem to have ended. You won. Your next step is to listen.

Listen for that slow rhythmic breathing. You'll hear your campers "pass out" one at a time. At last only two or perhaps three campers still have that mild restlessness. Safe? Almost.

Sit down on your bunk. If you have Old Squeaky, the campers will hear it. But they are listening for TWO squeaks, not one.

It takes one to sit and TWO to lie down. Just sit for another five minutes, then lie down with your eyes on that one camper that you are not sure about. Another five minutes and you are safe, but do NOT leave the cabin! The squeak of the door is the "GO!" signal to start another party because the counselor is gone.

Some counselors have come back to a cabin with the lights on, everyone up, and the remains of a pillow fight rather obvious. If you DO leave the cabin, leave someone else standing in the middle of the floor.

If you have seven- and eight-year olds, you may need to take a second trip to the bathroom about 30 to 60 minutes after "The End". When they finally slow down and relax, bed-wetting can be a real problem. With eight campers, you may have one to three with this problem.

One morning a young boy asked me, "Uncle Dave, didn't you go to bed last night?" I was standing in the middle of the cabin when he got up!

Obviously, after this routine has been established, you will be able to sack out much sooner. If you happen to have that rare ideal cabin, you can say "The End" and go to sleep yourself.

Some girls' cabins gather around on a couple of bunks for the story. If the girls are giving a high level of cooperation, that's fine. What has been herein described is the course to take when all is not so rosy.

Remember <u>Ecc. 5:12</u> "The sleep of a laboring man is sweet." Good night.

What to Do if Your Camper Wets the Bed — 2 Steps to Prevent it

Bedwetting, or enuresis, can ruin a camping experience for a child. If you have a camper with a history of bedwetting be calm, <u>do not</u> make the camper feel guilty. Handle the problem with a matter-of-fact attitude.

If a camper has had an "accident" during the night, he or she will be embarrassed. It is up to you to IMMEDIATELY take steps to alleviate the camper's anxiety. You should assist the bedwetter in as quiet and unobtrusive a manner as possible to change and air the bedding.

Care needs to be taken to prevent the bedwetter from becoming an object of ridicule in the cabin. Develop a signal so the bedwetter can comfortably ask you for help. Perhaps bedding can be changed or aired while your other campers are occupied elsewhere.

To prevent bedwetting:

1.   Limit liquid from supper on.

2.   Get the camper up 45 minutes to 1 hour after asleep and take him (or her) to the bathroom.

10   How to Work within the Organizational Chart

When you walk into camp, you have the right to expect that the Camp Director and supervisory staff have everything ready to go and are well organized. But whether this is the case or not, YOU have a job to do.

The point of this chapter is simple: Do your own job. Look back. That is a PERIOD after that sentence. DO YOUR OWN JOB, PERIOD.

The organizational chart may look something like this.

There is a Board of Directors at the top, then a Camp Director, then you as the counselor. In larger camps, it may be expanded with Assistant Directors, Program Directors, and so forth.

Someplace in all those little squares is one that says, "counselors". That's you. Who is just above you? That's the person you go to with your problems or if you need help.

Trouble

A problem comes in the course of the camp week, when you see someone else NOT doing the job they are supposed to do, or at least not doing it the way you think it should be done. Is that person just below you on the organizational chart? NO!

You have only two alternatives: go to the one that is immediately over you and express your concern, then DROP IT; or ignore it and go about your own business.

This may sound a little heartless or even uncaring, but what happens when this advice is not followed?

Let's assume that no one in camp follows this principle. Everyone's business is everyone else's business.

For example:

1.   During rest hour the counselor next to your cabin comes over and politely tells you to keep your campers quiet. (You were having a serious discussion on how to know if something is right or wrong and one of the kids said something that caused the others to laugh.)

You try to briefly explain this to your fellow counselor, but again his main concern is that rest hour be kept quiet. How do you feel right now toward that other counselor? How does he feel toward you? Is there peace and harmony and support and good feelings? I do not think the feelings are positive at all.

2.   Your camp uses the waitress system, in the dining hall. These girls serve the tables family style. You ask for another plate of pancakes, but she comes back with only two. You have a hungry table of campers! Only Two?!

Up to the kitchen you go with your plate and ask firmly for ten more pancakes. The dining room hostess tells you to sit down.

How do you feel toward that hostess and the waitress? How do they feel toward you? Is there peace and harmony and "<u>esprit de corps</u>"? Not quite!

How to Get the Most Out of Your Job

Each one in the camp has a special job to do. If that job is to be done effectively, each one must give his all to his own work.

There is a basic principle in the business world: if you are to succeed, major in one thing at a time.

If you are to be a successful counselor, major in your work of caring for the ones put in your cabin group.

Let the other staff members take care of their work. If they let down on their end of things and it affects you, you can go to your supervisor with your concern, and then ask for grace to continue to do your best with the way things are.

For example, the rest hour problem could be solved in the Director's office or in a staff meeting by coming to an agreement as to just what rest hour policy should be. Whatever is decided, live with it joyfully. The pancake problem could be solved with patience.

No one has died of hunger or starvation in a camp.

Words of encouragement to the other counselors, the waitresses, the Program Director and the Camp Director are always in order.

Many times you will see little things you can do to help (without interfering or taking over) other members of the camp family.

This leads to the last basic principle of organization. The fact that you are responsible for those below you on the organizational chart (i.e., the campers) is obvious, but did you know that you are ALSO responsible for those ABOVE YOU on that chart?

You are not responsible to correct or direct, but you are responsible to make them a success. If the Program Director is your boss, what can you do to make him a success? What can you do to help him do his job a little better? How can you make his job easier?

The answers to these questions would be something like this: "I can obey his instructions, do my very best, stay with my campers, never be critical of him, and keep him informed as to what is happening in the cabin."

If your mental attitude is one of support for the one over you, you will be amazed and happy at what you can do to help that person.

11 How to Have a Successful Cookout

Site Preparation

The cookout site itself needs to be prepared. Personally, I prefer just a place in the woods that is made by campers.

The campcraft books give excellent pictures and helps on how to make it safe, but basically, take precautions to keep the fire from spreading.

If in doubt, you are safer in making a hole and building the fire in a hole. This method holds the fire in a small area when there is wind, holds the coals together for better cooking, and makes it easier to put pots or pans over the fire by using two green sticks across the top of the hole.

When the cookout is over, it is easier to cover it all up safely so wind cannot fan the ashes.

The cookout site should also have a place to put the food, usually ten feet or more from the fire. Campers love to play around the fire, and rarely do they see their sneakers shoveling dirt into the food.

Don't yell at them; move the food! It is also handy to have a place, like a log, to sit down and eat. Keep the eating AWAY from the fire because plates that are set on the ground will surely end up with unplanned seasonings mixed in with the food.

A "Things to Include" Checklist

Before going on the cookout, you should have a check sheet. This is a written list of everything you will need on the cookout.

Do NOT rely on your memory or the experience of the cook. He has been doing it for five years. Check off everything in the box before you leave on the cookout.

If the cook or the ones packing the box used a check sheet, just go through the check sheet itself.

Things to include: adequate proportion of each food for the number going, correct number of plates, knives, forks, spoons, cups, napkins, cooking tools like large fork, spatula, pot or pan, HOT PADS, knife, matches (one of the most often forgotten items), extras such as salt, pepper, catsup, relish, and 1 gallon of water for extinguishing the fire. What is needed, will of course, depend on the menu. Think ahead.

How to Set Up When You Arrive

When you arrive at the cookout site, you need to get set up and then delegate responsibilities. If it is not a prepared site, make the fireplace, seating, cup hangers and so forth.

Your cabin may have taken an hour the day before to come and make the site a special place (see the campcraft books for the things you can do to really make it neat). Put the food a distance from the fire and make it clear that no one is to go into the food box except the counselor.

Now delegate the responsibilities: someone work with the counselor in setting up the food, others gather piles of firewood, two others get the fire going.

On cookouts, the prepared food is not near the fire. To serve, set it up cafeteria style with each one coming through the line to pick up his things. This system prevents wasting food and assures equal portions.

Sometimes, EVERYONE gathers firewood together. You want a large supply not far from the fire. Do not let more than two campers at a time work on the fire; it will go out with each one blaming the others.

Fire-Safety Tips

When children (and teens!) get a fire going, they apply the old axiom: bigger is better. This is the wrong place for that thought.

Keep control of how much wood is put on the fire. An old Peanuts cartoon has the little guy saying, "Ready for the hot dogs!" as he stands next to a fire eight feet tall!

A cooking fire is SMALL. The initial flames may reach a couple of feet, but the idea is to burn as much as you can as fast as you can to establish a pile of coals.

Wood should be the size of fingers, not as big as arms. If too much wood is put on, it will take too long to burn it all down.

If you are cooking with fry pan or pot, cooking can start as soon as the fire has a good start and has burned down enough to put the pot on. Again, go back to the campcraft books for illustrations.

The point here is to watch the campers so that the cookout fire does not become a bonfire or even a forest fire.

How to Get Your Campers Involved

Above all, when on a cookout, follow the basic principle that the CAMPERS <u>do what needs to be done</u>. They will NOT have a great experience if the old, "pro" counselor does it for them.

Let them make the fireplace area. Let them make the fire three or four times (it keeps going out). Let them cook the food. Make them clean up the mess. Let them put out the fire.

This is easier said than done. Sure, you will need to give them examples and show them how to do it, or do your own as an example. But let them do their own.

How to Keep the Spirit High

Keep a good spirit at the cookout. Rather than barking at a camper for digging into the food box, just remind him that it is off limits.

You may go hungry because you gave your hamburger to the camper who dropped his into the fire. (Usually the cook at home base will have mercy on you.)

Firebrands are always a problem, so just set the firm rule that sticks put into the fire, stay in the fire. You will have to keep one eye on the fire the whole time. **When**

all goes wrong, make light of it and build it up as an adventure.

Our group of boys had hiked to the hill several hundred yards from the home base.

The meal that I had planned (the whole camp was in cabin groups cooking this same meal) included corn on the cob roasted in tin foil and hamburger patties with potatoes and carrots and onion wrapped in tin foil and roasted. The corn was pre-wrapped. The hamburger was a "camper make your own" thing, so all the parts were sent. No tin foil for the hamburgers!

It was a beautiful day, and this was going to be a beautiful cookout.

Since I was the Camp Director and was supposed to be the expert, a solution had to be found. "Charlie, would you run back to the kitchen and get the tin foil? He soon came back with the message that tin foil was in all the boxes."

It was tempting to "pull rank" and demand it, but such would not be right. "O.K., how can I cook these hamburgers?" The corn! It was wrapped in foil! Carefully each boy unwrapped an ear of corn. The cookout went ahead with each boy getting his own meal ready. As soon as the hamburgers were done, we put the corn on the coals.

For you who have not done this, make sure the corn is in all its finest green coats and soak it well in water, then lay it on the coals and turn it over after ten minutes (unless it turns black before then!).

We took the corn out of the coals, unwrapped the green husks carefully, and feasted like kings. Sure, some were burned here and there, and some were not quite done, but so what!

The spirit of the whole thing was one of adventure and resourcefulness. No unkind words were spoken about the cook and no complaining about food. When a camper did say something, I responded with, "That's o.k., a little burned spot doesn't hurt. Just eat around it. Can you taste that special flavor from roasting it in the husks?"

Concluding a Cookout

Before leaving the cookout site, make sure all the garbage is picked up and stuffed into the cookout box or bag. Carry it back to the garbage cans, but FIRST separate out the cooking tools and silverware. A gallon of water is always brought for a fire extinguisher. Leave the area clean and neat and smokeless.

Experienced counselors have another saying that is used at the end of less than perfect cookouts: "Snack shop time is coming."

Whether it goes great or totally flops, have a good time with your campers and LET THEM DO IT. Keep the spirit high.

12   How to Have Manners in Camp

Camp is a friendly, informative, fun, and often light-hearted place. Young folks come to have a good time, meet friends, and learn new things. When at the table in the dining hall, eating is a special time of fellowship and frolic.

During a counselor training session before the camp season, I asked the counselors (who had been divided into small groups) to write down the answers to some specific questions on manners.

Keep in mind that at this camp we used only family-style dining. The following is the list of answers given to each question.

"What manners and courtesies can we expect of campers at the table?"

- Pass the food to the person to your right instead of reaching.
- Food is for eating, not for throwing or playing.
- Quiet talking is used instead of yelling.
- Remain seated at the table until dismissed.
- Wait to eat until everyone is served at your table.
- Share. Take only your portion. (In family-style eating, a platter of food should go all the way

around the table with everyone getting something before seconds are brought.)

- Everyone takes at least one "no-thank-you" portion. (In this camp, everyone had to eat at least a spoonful of what was served. Very often, after one spoonful, the camper wanted more.)
- Salt, pepper, and sugar containers are not toys.
- Use your fingers only for finger foods.
- Strictly observe the quiet rules. (When a small bell is rung, everyone is to become quiet.)
- Don't lean back in chairs.
- No elbows on the table.
- Put napkins in the lap and use them.

One might guess that the counselors who answered these questions had some experience. We can begin to see how having good manners is really just a way of being thoughtful and kind to others.

"What manners should be shown to the Director, Program Director, etc.?"

- Cooperate with them and encourage the campers to cooperate.

- Do not talk against them and joke against them.
- Give them respect.
- Keep campers under control. Quiet them down.
- Give them full attention.
- Ask them if there is anything that can be done for them.
- Help with the games or other activities.

"What manners and courtesy should campers show toward each other?"

- No pushing in line.
- Share the sports equipment.
- Be friendly.
- Include everyone in the games.
- Be willing to listen.
- Do not argue. Be agreeable.
- Help others with jobs to be done.
- Respect each other's property.
- Use each other's proper name.
- Be quiet while others are sleeping.

This particular list also gives some ideas to cover in cabin discussion periods. Can you see some problems that these counselors have faced in their experience with campers?

"What manners should the girls on staff show toward the other girls on staff?"

- Be quiet when others are sleeping. Some need to get that early afternoon rest.
- Respect other's property. Ask permission to borrow another's things and do not take advantage of them.
- Be polite.
- Don't criticize someone else's way of doing things.
- Don't gossip to or about them.
- Respect their feelings and beliefs.

Be realistic and don't go to extremes. Basically, that in itself is manners. If it is kind, it is good manners. How far should you go with manners?

That will depend on your cabin group. The little group of girls that just drips with honeyed sweetness will love your advice on how to develop more refined manners.

But those eleven-year old boys who are all body and no coordination will be doing well to keep the milk upright on the table, and to manifest enough self control to keep from pushing Peggy Pigtails out of line.

Camp is fun. If you can make manners fun, go as far as you can! If you have a difficult, or rather uncultured group, demand the minimum. You are the counselor.

13   How to Conduct Cabin Story Time

Probably the time that is most remembered in camp by both counselors and campers is that special time at the end of the day when the cabin finally quiets down and talks seriously about special matters. At least, it COULD be the best time of the day.

It is during this special end-of-day quiet time when you as the counselor can approach some delicate subject concerning behavior or attitudes that need to be changed.

You need to start planning what you will do long before you get to the cabin after the last activity of the day. Think through what you will do and how. Some counselors plan this out during rest hour or during some free time you may have during the day.

Four Steps to Successful Story Time

Step 1:   Establish a goal.

What do you want to accomplish? Is there an attitude among the group that needs to change? Is there a problem between campers that needs to be addressed? Is there a character weakness that needs to be challenged or strengthened?

If you are short on time or if you are working with a younger group who is dragging from a vigorous day, then keep this time short. Do a little something to just round out the day and wrap it up quickly.

However, if there is a need to reach a definite goal, take the time to plan out what you want to accomplish and how you want to accomplish it.

You need to keep your mind on a goal: with each sidetrack that campers take, definitely bring them back to the main track again. Without a goal in mind, you will not reach a destination within the time allotted by the camp schedule.

Even with a longer story time, the attention span of your campers at this time of night will have a very definite limit. Use your time wisely. Keep going toward your goal.

Step 2: Start!

When you start will depend on a combination of the clock and the state of readiness of your campers. As detailed earlier, in the going-to-bed routine, all the campers should be in bed at this point in time.

Sometimes you may have one or two stragglers who just can't get their act together. Do not wait for the last ones. Ignore them and get started anyway. Here is an example of how to jump right into it:

"Since most of you are ready for storytime, let's get started. We have a great story (or poem, or anecdote) tonight. Listen closely. Cathy, you crawl into bed as soon as possible, and quietly so the rest do not miss something. Many years ago there was a..." and you are into your story.

If you were going to use a discussion format, you could start something like this:

"While Cathy finishes up and gets into bed, let me ask the rest of you a question. Only one answer at a time, but I would really like to know what you think. If you were playing ball, like we were this afternoon, how would you feel if you struck out with the bases loaded?" (Your objective is to help the others see the need to encourage each other instead of cut down and criticize.)

Step 3:   Content.

What can you include in this storytime? What are some options for you to choose?

If you are going to use the discussion format, start with a fictitious story. Place the campers in the story as I did in the above example with a camper striking out with bases loaded. Then ask a question that will help them see from the perspective of the other person.

"How would you feel if...." is a good format to follow, but you will want to create others that fit into your objectives.

To do this, mentally go back through the day at camp. Recreate a general scene that MAY have happened. Do not retell what actually happened to one of your campers, because that would be very embarrassing and put him on the spot.

For the sake of helping your campers see it from the other's viewpoint, your fictitious story could take place anyplace — not just at camp: home, school, playground, gym, in a game, at the pool, etc.

If you are going to simply tell them a story, choose a story that has a moral or point or truth to it. You could introduce it with a general question like, "Why does it pay to be diligent (honest, fair, or generous...)?" Then tell the story. At the end you could answer your own question or open it up for discussion.

Step 4: The closing.

Be sure to plan to end with "The End" in order to bring the day to an official close. You can do this by turning out the lights at the end of the story and finishing up with your conclusion or a brief discussion in the dark cabin.

Be sure to make your goal or teaching clear at this point. If you have had a discussion, tie it all together.

Resources for a good Storytime

1. Check your camp library for story collections or chapter books. If your camp does not have a library and is near a town, check the public library for your old favorite adventure stories or ask the librarian for recommendations. Don't forget collections of Fairy Tales, Tall Tales and Etc.

2. Depending upon the age and level of sophistication of your campers, as well as their length of stay with you, it can be fun to read a chapter or two a night from a mystery series. Some popular examples are:

    The Boxcar Children Series by Gertrude C. Warner (gr.1-4)

    Nancy Drew books by Carolyn Keene (gr.3-6)

    Hardy Boys books by Franklin W. Dixon (gr.3-6)

    Alfred Hitchcock and the Three Investigators books (gr.3-6)

3. For Native American and wildlife stories and activities, Michael J. Caduto's two books are wonderful resources:

Keepers of the Earth: Native American Stories and Environmental Activities

Keepers of the Animals: Animal Stories and Wildlife Activities

4.   **The Animal Family** by Randall Jarrell (gr.2-6) is a poetic allegory of community.

5.   Don't forget poetry, especially nonsense verses! Jack Prelutsky and Shel Silverstein have wide appeal among children.

6.   **Sarah Bishop** and **Sing Down the Moon** by Scott O'Dell are two books featuring courageous heroines. The former is about a young girl at the time of the Revolutionary War and the latter describes a Navaho girl during the 1864 "Long Walk".

7.   Books with an outdoor theme that would appeal to the middle school age camper include Jack London's **White Fang** and **Call of the Wild**. The award winning **Hatchet** by Gary Paulsen is the story of a young boy who survives a plane crash and has only a hatchet.

8.   You will not find a beeter resource for true stories than **The Bible**. What happened many years ago is still a great teacher to kids today.

The following passages are examples of stories that can be read. Be sure to read the story ahead so it goes smoothly when you read to your cabin.

- **Psalms** — The whole book of Psalms is Hebrew Poetry. Just reading one chapter is a great way to end the day. These chapters can be meaningful to youth: 1, 4, 5, 8, 18:19-33, 19, 23, 34, 37:1-9, 40 91, 95, 100, 103:11-22, 112, 116, 119, 121, 127, 139, 145, 149, 150.

- **Proverbs** — This is a great book for you to study and then share appropriate parts with the campers. This book was originally written just for youth!

9.   Aesop's Fables have a long history of teaching youth. If you can bring a copy to camp with you, these very interesting stories never grow old and are great teachers.

☞ **The Lion and the Mouse.** (Little friends may prove great friends.)

☞ **The Crow and the Pitcher.** (Little by little will help you get what you need.)

☞ **The Hare and the Tortoise.** (Slow and steady wins the race. Don't Quit!)

☞ **The Shepherd Boy and the Wolf.** (People who tell lies are seldom believed when they do finally tell the truth.)

☞ **The Ant and the Dove.** (One good turn deserves another.)

☞ **The Dog and the Bone.** (The greedy often lose what they do have.)

If you Don't Have a Book

1. Use the creative energy of your campers and make up your own NIGHTLY CABIN STORY. Take the lead and start off with a sentence (on a dark and stormy night...) and go around the cabin, every camper adding another sentence until it is time for lights out or the story gets too twisted!

2. Another version of the "NIGHTLY CABIN STORY" is the "ADD A WORD" approach. This is most successful with the fast thinking ten year old campers or older as the story unfolds word by word as it moves from bunk to bunk.

3. "THE CAMP DUFFLE" is a good memory challenger which begins "I went to camp and in my duffle I packed..." This game also goes around the cabin with every camper adding yet another item to

the duffle, but also needing to correctly list all the preceding contributions.

14

How to
Lead a Discussion

What Not to Do

Have you ever played, "Guess what I'm thinking"? It's a game where the leader has the answer in mind and the others are trying to guess it.

Most people will not take the risk of being wrong; so no one will answer even the simplest question.

A good discussion leader must avoid any semblance of this game!

There are two things you must do.

- Encourage participation. The more campers participate together; the more interest, attention, and results will come from the study.

- Learn more about each camper. LISTEN with both ears and mind. Everything she says is telling you something about herself. By listening, you are beginning to understand where each camper is spiritually, mentally, socially, and emotionally.

Three Types of Camper
Response and What to Do with Each

The first is "The Talker." This person goes on and on and often just in circles. You will have to politely cut this person off, after giving him ample time to get his point across.

The second is the quiet one. He doesn't say anything, so ask him personally. "Terry, what do you think this man in the story was trying to do?" You might be amazed at how the quiet ones often come up with the greatest insights.

Third is the wrong answer child. He just can't seem to get on your track of thinking. Try to pick out the correct part of his response and repeat it with praise to the child who gave it. Or give him credit for being so close or for having a good idea.

In any case, NEVER be critical or call attention with any emphasis to his being wrong.

When a correct answer or response is given, give a clear word of praise or encouragement, then repeat the key phrase or sentence so everyone can hear it.

But when you repeat it, USE THE EXACT WORDS the camper used. Do not change anything or substitute any synonyms. Doing this adds great worth to the response and will greatly encourage others.

"Guess what I'm thinking of" puts worth only on the idea of the leader, rather than putting great worth on the ideas of those participating. The difference between these two approaches will make a vast difference in the amount of participation.

How to Get Kids Talking

If you want discussion, you need a question. The concern then becomes, "What kind of question?" We already buried "Guess what I'm thinking of", so let's move on to something that works.

Use an open-ended or opinion based question like "Who do you think is the greatest man in the Old Testament and why?" Each child may have someone else in mind. Praise each one for picking such a great man and repeat something of what the child gave for a reason of why he was great.

DO NOT end up with, "Those all are good, but I think the greatest man is David. David..." In so doing, you just shot down their worth and proved you were looking for a particular answer. The next time, they may not be so quick to answer you.

Instead, use this summary: "You have really chosen some great men: David, Samuel, Moses, Joseph — can you think of anything that was true about ALL of these men?" Can you put yourself as participant in this group and feel why you would be encouraged to participate? If you want to emphasize a particular point (as from the second question), you could say: "I like what you said about how each __. Can we be like that this week?"

Now you are guiding the discussion instead of killing it. You are not going back to preaching.

What to Do When It Does Not Work

Sometimes you can do everything right and nothing happens. There just is not the cooperation or interest or response or attention for which you hoped. Before putting yourself in the stocks, take a more objective look at the total situation. There may be other causes. For example:

1.   Are you wound up tight, disturbed, and thus not showing real love and concern for the campers? Your mind could really be on your home problems, girl friend problems, or other personal problems. The campers may pick up the tone and read, "He really doesn't care."

2.   You may be talking too much ("Perish the thought! How could THAT ever happen with

ME?"). You just need to stop long enough for them to think (don't let the silence scare you). Come back to the question method and wait patiently.

3.　　　　The campers may be wound up, excited, and not at all ready to settle down. This is often true on the first night and at weekend retreats. You can calm them down by reading a story (even OLDER ones like it).

On the first night, you will need time to go over the cabin rules and give your pep talk. If all else fails and the group just is not with you in your discussion or story, cut it short and have a shorter story time.

Send for help, too. The person just above you on the organizational chart should be available to help. In any case, do NOT scold and chastise or criticize the children; the supervisory staff is available to help you.

4.　　　　The children may be just too tired and have no energy left to listen by the end of the week. Put them to bed earlier and have a SHORT story time before the end, especially with younger children.

5.　　　　There may be something in the cabin that is keeping them going: mouse, fly, wasp, moth, spider, branch scratching the roof, night sounds in the woods. If you can't really get rid of the distraction, assure campers of care and protection, then turn the lights out and continue. Get their minds off it.

Again, put your pride in your pocket and send for help if you need it.

6.   You may have one or two campers who are definitely a problem. They have no discipline at home and are more or less continual trouble at camp. Now they are making storytime nearly impossible. Try solutions # 3, 4 or 5. Or, give a first warning and then a second, and the third time put them on the front steps of the cabin with a junior counselor.

I have had some campers "cool their heels" on the front step of the cabin for 45 minutes. Finally, they got bored with the peace and quiet and decided to go to bed peaceably.

For most problems there is a solution. Work with your fellow staff members as a team to find just the right solution for your situation. Give your best to the campers by getting the help you need.

15 How to Understand Camper Personalities

Four Basic Factors

There are four basic factors that generate behavior patterns. Each one is significant, but each child is a special and unique mix of all four. In any one child, you may find <u>one</u> factor that dominates all the others.

The four factors are:

- Behavior that is characteristic of a given age group.

- Behavior that is learned from the cultural and family context.

- Behavior patterns growing out of the birth order sequence in the family unit.

- Behavior patterns that are characteristic of a personality type.

How Age-Group
Characteristics Affect Your Campers

Some books or booklets have age-group characteristic charts. This is a list of things common for each general age of children.

These charts can be quite helpful, but as a counselor, I had problems remembering the lists!

If you have such a chart and it helps you, great! With or without such a list, the following project will become more meaningful than pre-made charts.

How to Profile
Each of Your Campers

At the beginning of each rest hour when the campers are quieting down, or during some other quiet time during the day when you can observe your campers, take out a clipboard and piece of paper. Make a list of the common behavior patterns that you have noticed in your group of campers.

If you have a wide age span in the same cabin group, make a separate list for each age. You will begin to notice things that are common to most of the children of any given age.

For example, your list may include things like this: giggles a lot, stays in groups of three, rarely alone, looks to the others for approval, works hard, cooperative, anxious to please, very noisy, continually active. You may be amazed at how much they all act alike!

If you will do this project and add to it each week, your real understanding of children will take a huge jump. As you understand them more, you will have more patience.

You will also have the ability to spot the exception, the troubled child, the immature, the advanced, the leader, and the late bloomer.

Compare notes with other counselors who have the same age of camper, on your day off or between camp sessions. It will be a lot of fun and a giant learning experience.

If you are a college student, this project will be good for a super term paper in the Childhood Development course.

How Culture and Family Affects Your Campers

Cultural and family background may have a major impact on a child's behavior. If a child grows up in the big city, his interests, language, values and experiences may be quite different from the well-off suburban child. How do you think a divorce in the family would impact a child? Is your camper from an ethnic group that is strong in tradition or special values?

Many of these answers can be found by listening and observing from the time you first meet the camper and parents. Once you understand this background, the camper's behavior will become more understandable.

One key factor that you want to learn through observation, listening, and perhaps from the registration information is the possibility of major traumatic experiences in the child's past.

Such experiences may include continual fear from city gangs, a divorce between parents, the death of a parent, parental abuse, parental neglect, overdose of TV, school failure or other troubles, and significant sibling rivalry or abuse.

These kinds of things often produce a marked insecurity in the life of a child.

The child will handle this insecurity by forming some type of behavior pattern that shields him from further hurt. Dr. James Dobson in his book, <u>Hide or Seek</u>, goes into great detail describing the many alternatives.

The basic thesis of the book is that a child will either learn to run away and hide (try not to be noticed, stay out of the way), or he will seek (be aggressive, act out, be pushy, angry).

When you meet a child that tends to go toward either extreme, be sensitive to the possibility that this child is hurting but trying to cover it up.

The principle for you to remember is that children that are basically insecure need CONSISTENCY in love and discipline. Every child needs loads of unearned love.

The behavior-problem child needs clear rules that are consistently maintained. This is easy to say, but you will need God's special grace to carry out this super-human task.

How Birth-Order
Sequence Affects Your Campers

FIRST BORN

Closely related to family background are the significant patterns associated with birth-order sequence. Studies in birth-order patterns major in the first (oldest) child in the family.

This child often tends toward being a perfectionist, reliable, conscientious, well-organized, critical, serious, an achiever, legalistic, loyal, self-reliant and a people pleaser. Take the time to learn this list. You will see strong evidences of it in your campers.

The reason for these common characteristics is not so much genetic as it is in the parental handling of the first born. She is given an exorbitant amount of attention, high expectations, and much praise right from the time he could smile.

For a first born, any one of the above characteristics could become dominant because of the parental attention.

LAST BORN

The last born (youngest) may also evidence some strong and noticeable characteristics. If the parents and siblings treated this child as the baby of the family, he may become outgoing, affectionate, absent-minded, and uncomplicated.

This last born is often the clown that thrives on attention.

Their behavior can also experience a wide swing from being so loving and affectionate to being rebellious, critical, spoiled, impatient and impetuous. This behavior swing from one extreme to the other is often "normal" for this child.

These behavior patterns have been created because he was never taken seriously, or perhaps he was always seen as the smallest and weakest and youngest. So he compensates by attracting attention or by trying to prove himself to adults.

Note, however, that these children are often people-oriented and can be sensitive to others. With their focus on people and relationships, things in their lives get lost: "Where are my books? Did he take my toothbrush? Where's my other sock?"

THE MIDDLE CHILD

The key to every child after #1 is born is the sibling directly above him in line. Each child tends to be in competition with the one who is next oldest. He may try to copy or try to catch up with the older brother or sister. More often, he will try to be the opposite. If the older sibling is "Miss Maturity," this child may show little or no interest in grown-up things. If the older one is athletic, this child may either be super competitive or stay clear of all athletics.

Usually, this second child is competitive in some way (trying to prove himself) and wants to avoid conflict (a peace maker). When you have a middle child, gently probe to find out something about his next oldest brother or sister.

Listen for clues as to whether your child is jealous, rebellious, competitive or in harmony with this older one. You will want to note how your camper compares himself in interest and abilities.

Not all children fit these general patterns of birth order. Many have a complex mix because of divorce, being the youngest child but oldest boy (or girl), being second or third but also the oldest in the "second family," and so forth.

In other words, birth-order significance is not always clear and a usable tool to help you understand a child. Use the birth-order significance only when you have a clear case, which is usually the oldest or youngest child.

For a complete treatment of birth-order significance, read The Birth Order Book by Dr. Kevin Leman.

Four Basic Personality Types

The fourth factor for understanding children is the personality type study. Like the birth-order study, a child who is STRONG in only one type will be easiest to spot. Most children are a mix and therefore more balanced.

The following chart is a clear and abbreviated outline of the four basic personality types. It will help you know what to look for in children.

However, the younger the child, the more his behavior will be more in line with age group characteristics. <u>This chart is most applicable to older teens and adults.</u>

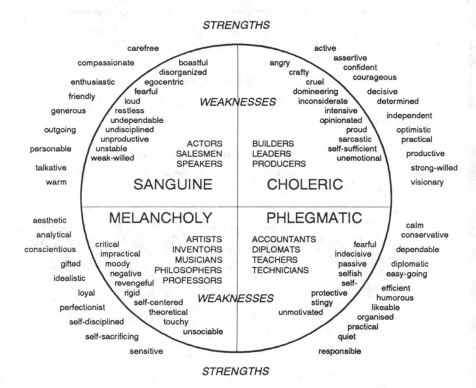

If one of your campers (or fellow camp staff!) is clearly in one of the quarters on the chart, you have a wealth of understanding of that person.

If you are clearly on the opposite side of the chart, can you see why this person can be completely normal and yet so unlike yourself?

It is so natural to expect others to see things the way we do, but a basic understanding of personality types will help us see that each person is unique. One type of person is NOT better than another.

Use the chart to better understand your campers and yourself, and help you accept each one just the way he is.

I regret not being able to give proper recognition to the one who created this chart. It was given to me many years ago by a friend.

For a full explanation of personality types, read <u>Spirit Controlled Temperaments</u> by Tim LaHaye, Tyndale House Publishers.

An Example of Personality Types

Let's put all this together with one hypothetical example.

Bouncy Benny bounds into the cabin. Benny is friendly, not shy, a little fearful, and looks neat. The parents obviously are middle class and well-mannered. (You can guess that he has had good upbringing. He may fit into the Sanguine type.)

The parents introduce themselves, but when you check Benny's last name, you notice the parent's last name and Benny's last name are not the same. (You now realize that there has probably been either a divorce or death. There could be emotional scars and behavior patterns that try to cover up the hurts.)

In the getting-to-know-you conversation that comes the first day of camp, you find that Benny is the youngest of three children. You conclude that Benny has the potential for being the spoiled baby of the family.

Before you label Benny as a spoiled, self-centered Sanguine who is basically insecure, you would do well to observe and listen carefully. He may NOT fit the picture.

If he does prove to fit the picture, at least you will have a much greater understanding of why he acts the way he does. As you work with Benny, remember the basic principle: children tend to live UP to our

expectations or to live DOWN to our expectations.
NEVER label a child and then expect the worst.

Conclusion

It is really exciting to see every child as a very
special person with a unique combination of these four
critical factors.

As we begin to thus understand each camper, the
approach we take and the expectations we put forth will
vary with each one.

Even for those many children who are a blend of
these many possibilities, we can expect them to NOT fit
the mold that formed them as they were developing
children. Each one will indeed be different.

16

How to Make that Last Night of Camp "A Time to Remember"

For the youngest junior age campers, the last night of camp "has finally come." These little people are anxious to see Mom and Dad the next day. They may also be very tired from being on-the-go all week. In some camps, it works well for this youngest age group to go to bed earlier than the others because they are so beat.

For the grade school age child, that last night comes upon him all too quickly. "You mean we have to go home ALREADY"? They feel as though they could just take up permanent residence in camp! On that last night their adrenalin may be flowing more and thus they are evidencing more activity; or they may be dragging from having had a wonderful, but exhausting week.

If you have a super active group, calm them down by your tone of voice, your mannerisms, and your conversational topics. "Jim, what did you like BEST about this week"? Get one thinking instead of acting, and you'll begin to get the attention of the others.

You want to draw attention to what was learned in classes, new songs which were learned, and any noticeable ways that lives were changed.

For the junior-high and high-school age group, their thinking may be taking a whole different turn. Initially, they may have thoughts about never seeing that special friend "ever again."

Emotionally, for teenagers, a parting of ways is always forever. They have not yet experienced the wonderful ways in which we are brought back together again.

Some young minds may also be thinking of the one grand climactic practical joke which they can play (this depends a lot upon the type of camp). If this describes your cabin group, you may need to use some of the "The End" methods in chapter 9 and alert your supervisor so extra help will be available.

Your objective is to get their minds on what was done this week in camp. Have them share good experiences or tell what was most meaningful to them this week. End your time with praise, and then challenge them by saying something like this:

> "Sometimes it is tempting to end a week of camp by cutting lose or playing practical jokes on others, but that would put a sour ending to a very sweet week. It would be wrong to wreck it."

Another problem in some camps is the boy-girl relationships. Perhaps your camp has maintained a no-dating standard, or maybe the director has allowed very close friendships to develop.

The guys or gals in your cabin may have their imaginations running away with them: "I've got to see him tonight. We can sneak out after the counselor is asleep."

If you sense this happening, talk to them like this: Tomorrow is the appropriate time to have the good-byes. Rather than think of this as the LAST time you will see him/her, think about when the next time might be."

It might be good to talk about "How do two friends part?" You can guide the discussion into covering such topics as talking together, writing and encouraging, and maintaining standards (mutual respect).

The Last Night for the Staff

Some camps make the last night of camp for the staff a very special time. You will need to do all that you can to bring the summer's season to a fitting close. Gather together several ideas (on paper to help clarify and abbreviate your ideas) of what was done through your work or in your life this summer.

You need to still be the leader. Don't let down your guard on this last night. Make the ending of camp a friendship high, not a grand blow-out.

A big, last-night party and a lowering of standards is often a normal temptation. On the last night of camp, you need to encourage the other staff members to follow your lead.

Get names and addresses and start the habit of writing to others. You now know many needs, so now you can care effectively.

Write to these friends and let the friendships grow. An old song says, "Make new friends but keep the old, one is silver and the other gold." I have found this to be true.

17 Little Extras to Make You Super Effective

This chapter will collect all the little odds and ends to make you an effective counselor. It may be one of the most important chapters in this whole book!

How to Be a Good Example

The camp cannot afford a bad example in the counselor's position. If the camp director is perceptive, he will give such a person a one way ticket home rather than risk the wrong lessons in the cabin family.

Being the example is no longer a cheap motivation or trick but becomes an absolute necessity. We tell our campers to do right, but do they see you struggling with problems or being rebellious against authority?

We tell them to be quiet in class and rest hour, but are we talking or passing facial messages to friends?

We tell them to sing, but can they even hear you when you are right next to them? (So you have a voice that sounds bad even in the shower, let everybody hear it, and the camper will give singing a try, too.)

So like it or not, you DO have the responsibility to be the example.

Fun in the Kitchen

It sure looks like it, but the camp kitchen is NOT the place for counselors. Sometimes you see all that food going back and your table was a little short. It is so tempting to find an excuse to spend a little time in there. But are you an exception? Can others go there, too? Probably it's against the camp rules.

Every person who goes into the kitchen carries with him just a little more dirt, a few more germs, and probably leaves behind a healthy dose of confusion. Let the cook be a good guy. Don't even ask to be an exception.

How to Set the Spirit

You have had a hard morning. Lunch is late. At last you get to the head of the serving line. Then you see it. Burned grilled cheese again! You don't need to say a thing, your face is as clear as the T.V. screen.

What will the campers do? Probably they will pick up on your signal and reflect, "Yuck! Who can eat that stuff!" You set the spirit. What could you do to create a beautiful spirit at that disappointing moment?

The camp schedule has a few minutes of free time before lunch. That special someone happens to be in the play area at the same time. You also see Larry Lonesome standing by himself. He's your camper. What will you do? O.K., what SHOULD you do?

A great camp spirit is created when each person gives of himself to others. A selfless and self-giving spirit makes a great camp spirit.

What to Do about Practical Jokes

For some reason, "practical" jokes seem to just burst out all over in some camps. Someone starts it and creates a good laugh. Another one picks it up; then there is some retaliation — do him one better. And so it grows and grows. The "joke" is usually at someone else's expense. Very often it involves some destruction of property.

One summer such a spirit got moving in camp. Then one morning the young man who was helping with maintenance saw his prize running shoes cut to shreds and hanging from the flag pole. Funny? Not at all. He was furious and very hurt. If this spirit of "practical" jokes gets started in your camp, <u>kill it</u>.

If the joke is on you, accept it and then let it die without any retaliation. Most of these jokes are only a low way for one person to take out bad feelings toward another person. They do not belong in camp.

Some camps have a tradition of playing jokes on the counselors. This can be done, but carefully. Such all-camp fun needs to have these criteria:

- It is for the campers' benefit.

- It shows the campers how to be good sports (the example of the one getting it).

- It can be an element in building unity as we play together.

- Such jokes are ALWAYS mild, never painful and never destructive.

An example would be the camp skits where someone gets a little wet in the "punch line."

Seven Sacrifices You May
Need to Make for Your Campers

Why are you at camp, anyway? The answer is obvious: to minister to the campers. Even though this is not new, <u>keep this thought coming back to your mind again and again.</u> Have patience with the Director and thank him for reminding you of this repeatedly all summer.

- If camp is for the camper, your social life comes SECOND to that of time spent with the children.

- If food runs short in the dining hall, you are the one to go without.

- If the campers are lined up, you are last in line.

- If there is a fun activity going on, your job is to see that your children have a blast.

- If there is a ball game, you hit the ball only if all the other children have had a turn.

- If there is a contest, you step aside and let the campers compete, even if it means your team may lose.

- When lunch is dismissed, you don't tarry to talk, you move out with your kids.

Counselor Exhaustion —
How to Prevent It

This problem can really undermine the effectiveness of the counselor. Even with the number one problem under control, this thing can wipe you out. <u>The problem is exhaustion</u> — Dr. Dave will give his prescription.

- REST during rest hour. Let the other counselor take the campers or get a relief person to fill in for you.

- SLEEP AT NIGHT. Believe it or not, you will not feel like going to bed. Quite often you want to stay up later, talk, socialize, or read.

- Take a good dose of strong multiple vitamins every day. I have found the Shaklee plan to work well.

- Have a counseling session with the Director of the camp, and perhaps the camp nurse. Do not push yourself to the end, because then you are no good to anyone. Do not let pride take you on a dead-end road of self-destruction. Take care of yourself so you can take good care of the children entrusted to your care.

What to Do When It Rains

The barometer which tells whether the day will be sunny or cloudy is the expression on your face. SMILE and look for special opportunities when it rains.

Whatever your situation, follow these basic principles:

- Never say a discouraging word. It will "dry up" the fun.

- Be positive, both inwardly and outwardly.

- Be prepared with an hour of activity in the cabin. It may take the camp staff a while to adjust.

- Listen carefully for special announcements over the camp's P.A. system or bell system.

- Remember, the camper is here for only five full days. We cannot afford to miss ONE day because of rain. Let's make the most of it.

- Check the book, "The Camp Counselor's handbook of Over 90 Games & Activities Just for Rainy Days" by David Burrow.

What to Do if You
Fall in Love at Camp

Is it wrong to fall in love in camp?
One could hardly call such a great feeling and flutter of
the emotions sinful. The problem is, how do two people
handle it?

The problem is so real and so very difficult, that in
my multiple years of camp ministry, I have witnessed
only a handful of couples who could really handle the
whole problem well. How did they do it?

- They set their priority on their campers. When
  it was time to be with the campers, they were
  with their campers.

- They earnestly sought self-control to control
  their feelings and the temptation to spend time
  together, instead of in their duty to children.

- They planned ahead. They found "loop holes"
  in the camp schedule when they could be
  together. For example, with some effort they
  arranged to have the same time off. Sometimes
  they were partners in teaching the same class to
  campers. If one really tries, he might even get
  his cabin of boys assigned a table close to her
  cabin of girls. Planning can really pay off.

- Maintain a no-physical-contact policy. When the relationship goes into holding hands, kissing, and embracing, the emotions and inner drives become jet engines too big to keep under real control.

- Agree together how to do it. Set mutual policies.

More often than not this situation is not ideal. The couple are like two magnets. Somehow they always manage to be together.

The Director is quite suspicious that someplace a duty is not being performed. When a Director sees a guy counselor and girl counselor at the drinking fountain and no campers around, he knows 16 children are being short-changed, and the potential for trouble in those cabins is very high.

Why are you at camp? To find a girl or boy friend? If the heterosexual relationship is your priority, then it's time to pack your bags.

Campers did not come to camp to see the staff pair off. Parents did not pay hard-earned money to send their children so the staff can find their "someone special."

The camp board did not spend hours of time and assume great responsibility so our counselors could spend most of the day chatting about nonessentials and griping over the Director's harassment.

What to Do if a Camper has a Crush on You

A word should be added about another love affair in camp — the camper who flips over a counselor or staff person. Such an occurrence can have a large measure of humor in it for the staff. But be careful of the child's very real feelings and needs.

As with any behavior, we must ask, "Why?" We can only guess that perhaps this child is starved for love, or perhaps she has been accelerated in sexual interests by T.V., love stories and older sisters.

Whatever the reason, we want the best for that child, and the path he or she has taken for fulfilling their need is NOT the best. In short, don't encourage it. Be polite and kind and gentle, but do not approve of the crush.

What to Do when You find out a Camper has been Abused at Home

It may be when they are changing for swimming that you notice your camper has a number of bruises or other marks. It could be late in the week and after your camper has gained confidence in you that he/she confidentially tells you about major trouble in the home. You might even have another camper tell you about another camper in your cabin who has been molested by Dad.

What you should **NOT** do:

1. It's juicy gossip and makes a great story to tell the other counselors. Resist the temptation. To spread such stories around is to add one more blow onto your camper. He has had enough already. Please, do not add to the hurt.

2. Do not play the part of Judge. It is not up to you to find out the details and truth of the story. Remember, some kids get in fights with other kids, so those marks and bruises might well be from such a fight rather than child abuse at home.

    Child abuse is "popular" and creates a lot of attention for a child; could it be that the stories the CHILD is spreading are false?

3. Please do not try to counsel the child concerning this problem. The hurts, emotions and feelings run very deep. Child abuse takes special counseling.

What you **Should DO**:

1. Take extra care to be sensitive to the child's feelings and thoughts. Some counselors like to horse around a little with their campers, but for an abused child this may be too close to a horror scene from real life at home.

2. Take the problem seriously. It may be a misunderstanding on your part, but it is better to not take that chance. If there is the possibility of child abuse, act accordingly.

3. If the child needs your firm arm around the shoulder (younger girls love to hold hands with the counselor), give what is needed. Do not be afraid to give wholesome love and attention. But at the same time, do not force it on the child.

4. Lean heavy on the other campers to mind their own business if one of them sees marks and begins to give a child a hard time. Come to the defense of the child and draw attention to some other subject.

5. Report your observations or suspicions to the camp director. Genuine child abuse, in most states, must be reported according to the law. This is NOT the job of the counselor, but of the camp director. The Director may want to

involve the Camp Nurse, but that is his/her decision and not yours.

What to Do if Your Supervisor Wants a Conference — with YOU

There are plenty of things that the one over you (let's just say the Director) would like adjusted in some way. (S)He may notice that you are scowling when getting the kids lined up for lunch. (S)He may have been bothered that you did not sing (set the example) last night. ((S)He doesn't know about the very sore throat you have been fighting.) Maybe (s)he has heard about the rift between you and the counselor in the cabin next door and wants to get it straightened out.

Whatever the reason for the interview, take three steps to avoid getting a bad attitude over it.

- Stop and think before jumping to your own defense. Is there any truth in it? Do I need to change something I am doing? Perhaps you need only to explain the situation, like the sore throat.

- Be thankful that someone cares enough to help you. Do what is asked. Now move on with the duty you have been given. Don't dwell on it and make a federal case out of it.

- If you were misunderstood, try to talk it over
  with the Director. You may need to change the
  outward appearance. If you still feel you are
  right, let it go. Now MOVE ON.

How Much Sleep Should You Get?

Some experts now say that teenagers need at least
eight hours of sleep each night. But you say, "I don't
FEEL that need."

True, most teens can go on five to seven hours a
night for several days, BUT THEN, suddenly, they are
out of energy. They are also "out of sorts" and impatient.
Colds come more easily, as do problems. What
happened? You can run on reserve energy for many
days, but when it is gone, IT'S GONE! You can find
yourself near fatigue, exhaustion, or even infectious
mononucleosis.

Rather than make the decision based on feelings,
aim for the full eight hours every night. Save that reserve
energy for emergencies when you'll need it.

Even with eight hours a night, in a full camp
routine, you will be using up your energy, but use it
slowly. Be at your best right to the last day of camp.

18 How to Love Your Campers

If I, as a counselor or staff person, speak like one of the great orators when I feel inspired, or even if I should be as eloquent as an angel, but don't have that heart-deep love for the child to whom I am speaking, I'm just blaring like a trumpet in a junior high band, or banging like a kitchen cook on a pot to make symphonic music.

Or if I could foretell the future events in the lives of these campers and really understand the answers to the deep questions the children ask, and if I could have such great trust and belief in God that I could move mountains, but really don't have a sincere love for those to whom I am supposedly ministering; I'm not a great person. Actually, I'm nothing, less than the smallest or most rebellious child.

If I give away everything I own to the poor children who come, and if I completely wear myself out, or should die in saving a young life; if I should do all this without love for my campers, it is of absolutely no profit to me.

So what is love? How can I make my oratory and abilities and sacrifices really pay off and be worth something?

Love is putting up with the slow camper because he just can't do any better, or perhaps has never been motivated to try.

Love is looking for the little extra things to do or to say to my cabin full of campers.

When I love my campers, I'm not jealous when they prefer one another's company to mine. I'll just rejoice at the good friendships they are making.

Because I love these children, I'll not brag about my abilities or education or experience during cabin devotions. I'm more interested in them and what they think about.

Love is speaking to a camper on his level and avoiding the pedestal relationship.

Even though they are children, love is treating them with good manners and courtesy. Love is sharing my life and sometimes my things.

Love is a calm word and an orderly response to four children clamoring for my attention at the same time.

Love is not keeping track of the wrongs that campers do, because I've forgiven them.

Love is being unhappy when one of my children wrongs another, and love is rejoicing when the truth is known.

One of the great things about love is that I can overlook the multitude of faults that each child has because I see the good that each child is trying to achieve.

Love means I can really trust that child, even though she may have let me down several times already.

Love gives me a vision of all that this precious child CAN be.

And lastly, love keeps me going 'till the end of camp so that every one of my children receives the very best of me.

19   What You Need to Know When Everything Keeps Going Wrong

They assigned you a cabin, the one with the leaky roof.

Then in walked your Junior Counselor, Fanny Flighty. She couldn't figure out if she should put on a coat first or her shoes.

When you sat down in the dining hall, your chair collapsed. Your table was the last one to be served the spaghetti — cold.

When you asked for seconds (hoping it would be hot), they said, "We just ran out."

Then the Director asked you to lead a song at the meeting, the only song you did not know.

By the first night you knew your cabin of campers were all angels — complete with horns and tails.

The first week you were chosen by an anonymous kangaroo court to be the first one to take a pre-breakfast dip in the lake (the ice melted off just two weeks ago).

The second week was the same as the first, only perhaps a little worse.

Two of your campers must be rejects from the youth reformatory because they seem well educated in evil tricks and foul language.

Yours is the only cabin that scores perfectly for cabin cleanup; you never passed once all week.

In riflery, the B.B. guns never worked, until your boy aimed at that girl walking by.

It did not rain all week, until it was your turn to conduct games after supper.

On the cookout they would not stop putting more wood on the fire. The other cabin of boys put out the forest fire before it reached the pine grove.

The third week, fourth week, fifth week, sixth week all were equally exciting. Nothing went right. You always got the worst cabin in camp. "Why me"? you asked repeatedly.

You begin to wonder if camp is some kind of penance punishment.

My second summer as a counselor was something like this fictitious experience, but not really that bad. For about five weeks I wondered why my cabin was always the worst one. Finally, I went to the Program Director who was the one assigning campers to cabins.

I asked why I always got the worst ones. He told me: "I know a lot of the kids because they have been here before. I give you the worst ones because you can handle them." That was great for my ego, but as I walked back to the cell, uh, cabin, I was thinking: "Isn't someone else able? I don't think I'm doing all that great with the boys."

It was years later before I realized what had happened. I was being prepared for a life work with children.

By giving me child after child with problems, God was teaching me how to work with them and how to help them. If all had gone smoothly, many lessons would not have been learned.

If you find yourself always getting the worst, rejoice that God has a very special plan for your life which is the very best! He is teaching you what most others will never learn.

You are someone special.

20 Child Abuse — How to Spot it and What to do about it

It's been growing at alarming rates all across the country. According to a study done by the Los Angeles Times, as many as 13 million children (8 million girls and 5 million boys) will be abused before age 18.

You may have one or more of these children in your cabin.

Don't panic, you've got plenty of support here at camp to help you deal with this problem.

Unless the child has come right out and told you of one or more specific incidents, please use the following list as a **GUIDE ONLY.**

Remember, some of these symptoms may underlie other problems beside child abuse (i.e. lack of appetite may be because of homesickness).

10 Common Symptoms of Sexual Abuse

1.   Explicit (sometimes bizarre) sexual knowledge

2. Precocious sexually related experimentation or speech

3. Obsession with masturbation

4. Withdrawal from normal human contact

5. Suicidal depression; self-destructive tendencies

6. Loss of appetite (normal day one of camp)

7. Unexplained bruises or injuries in genital areas

8. Lack of self-esteem or self-worth

9. Frequent nightmares

10. Infections of the mouth, gums or throat (Be vigilant for venereal disease of the anus or throat. Incidents are no longer uncommon in children.)

NOTE: These are <u>symptoms</u> and they <u>may</u> <u>not</u> indicate a problem. So procede with extreme caution! It is vitally important to your camper's welfare that you stay alert without becoming paranoid!

It may be when they are changing for swimming that you notice your camper has a number of bruises or other marks. It could be late in the week and after your camper has gained confidence in you that he/she confidentially tells you about major trouble in the home. You might have one camper tell you about another camper in your cabin who has been molested by Dad.

3 Things NOT to do

1.   <u>Please do not try to counsel the child concerning this problem</u>! Don't take the risk of doing more harm than good! The hurts, emotions and feelings run very deep. Child abuse takes special care in counseling. Be a good listener and be sure to show compassion. Let the child confide in you. The child obviously has to get this burden "off his shoulders".

2.   It's juicy gossip and makes a great story to tell the other counselors. Resist the temptation. Spreading such stories around only adds one more blow onto your camper. He has had enough already. Please, do not add to the hurt.

3.   Do not play the part of Judge. It is not up to you to find out the details and truth of the story. Remember, some kids get into fights with other kids, so those marks and bruises might well be from such a fight rather than child abuse at home.

Child abuse is "popular" and creates a lot of attention for a child; could it be that the stories the CHILD is spreading are false?

5 Things to do Right Away

1.   Take extra care to be sensitive to the child's feelings and thoughts. Some counselors like to horse around a little with their campers, but for an abused child this may be too close to real life horror at home.

2.   Take the problem seriously. It may be a misunderstanding on your part, but it is better to not take that chance. If there is the possibility of child abuse, act accordingly.

3.   If the child needs your firm arm around the shoulder (younger girls love to hold hands with counselor), give what is needed. Do not be afraid to give wholesome love and attention. But at the same time, do not force it on the child.

4.   Lean heavy on the other campers to mind their own business if one of them sees the marks and begins to give the child a hard time. Come to the defense of the child and draw attention to some other subject.

5.   **Report your observations or suspicions to the Camp Director.** Genuine child abuse, in most states, must be reported according to the law. This is NOT the job of the counselor but of the Camp Director. The Director may want to involve the Camp Nurse, but that is his decision and not yours.

For more detailed information contact:

Child Protection Program
7441 Marvin D. Love Freeway, Suite 200
Dallas, TX 75237
(214) 709-0300

The Three-Minute Daily Review Sheet

- **Stay with your campers.** Let the others horse around if they must, but don't leave your responsibility. Give your children all you can. Buy every minute. Never, never, never leave them alone.

- **Press for help when you need it.** If the director lets you down, work out an assistance plan with the Program Director or even the counselor next door. "When my kids are heard by your kids after lights out, come on over to my cabin and read the riot act. Then I'll do the same for you." ANY outside person carries a special weight of authority. Use it.

- **Don't try to change the camp.** Major on your kids and do your job. Let the camp go as it is. Being a counselor takes all you have.

22 How to Measure Your Success

They are gone! Whether between camp sessions or after the last day of the last week, you are suddenly struck by the stark quietness. It is all over. Camp has ended. Were you a success? Did you do well?

Even if your camp has an effective evaluation program that will help you know, this list of questions will be a good self-test to help you measure your success.

Think back on the past week or the whole summer. Rate yourself: 1 = Very Low; 5 = Very High.

1. Did I give my best to my campers?   1 2 3 4 5

2. Did I give each camper adequate time? 1 2 3 4 5

3. Did I stay WITH my campers?   1 2 3 4 5

4. Did I care for every camper every day? 1 2 3 4 5

5. Was I NOT bossy with my campers?   1 2 3 4 5

6. Did I counsel with every camper
    one-on-one?   1 2 3 4 5

7. Were my story times at night camper-centered and without preaching?   1 2 3 4 5

8. Did I maintain my own health?   1 2 3 4 5

9. Did I maintain a consistent example?   1 2 3 4 5

10. Did I get along well with the other staff? 1 2 3 4 5

11. Did I fully support my supervisor and the Camp Director?   1 2 3 4 5

12. Did I meet needs that were NOT my direct responsibility?   1 2 3 4 5

13. Was I positive and encouraging?   1 2 3 4 5

14. Did I do something to improve my skill as a counselor?   1 2 3 4 5

15. Did I complete the camp's required evaluations, forms, reports, and so forth? 1 2 3 4 5

16. Did I leave my cabin or living area
     clean?   1 2 3 4 5

17.   1 2 3 4 5

18.   1 2 3 4 5

19.   1 2 3 4 5

20.   1 2 3 4 5

For numbers 17 to 20, add the things that are expected of you in your camp this summer. Checking yourself each week will be very beneficial in increasing your camp ministry effectiveness.

How to Play It Safe

Check List

The campers came to have a good time. The camp organization wants each to experience growth. Both of these objectives can be destroyed if there is an accident.

If a camper steps on a nail, breaks a bone, becomes seriously ill or experiences a large cut that requires hospital care, that camper is out of all camp activities for part or all of the camp period.

Careless Cal, the cool counselor, takes his kids on a dangerous climb up rugged cliffs. He has a monkey swing contest in the cabin rafters. He didn't control the firebrands (burning sticks) the campers waved around during the cookout. The milk drinking contest at lunch put two kids in the infirmary. By the end of the week it was hard for him to measure results because so many in his group missed whole days of camp.

The Camp Director requires safety to accomplish both camp and camper goals and to keep the high cost of insurance down.

Counselors, like Careless Cal, do not think about these things; they only want everyone to have a good time.

You are the greatest factor in keeping that balance between having fun and playing it safe.

It is you who is right there with the camper most of the day.

It is your responsibility to prevent accidents by keeping one step ahead of the campers and THINKING, because the campers will not think safety.

As the days and weeks whiz past, slow down enough to check over the following list once or twice a week.

A safe camp will largely depend on a safety-thinking counselor.

In the Cabin or Living Quarters

**Okay   Needs
         Help**

___   ___   Are <u>all</u> exit doors clearly marked and working?

___   ___   Is there a fire extinguisher handy and updated?

___	___	Are extension cords properly used?
___	___	Are there no sharp edges to run into?
___	___	Do you prevent running or horseplay?
___	___	Are the electrical circuits not overloaded?
___	___	Are there any heating devices near combustibles?

General

Okay   Needs Help

___	___	Do you know what to do in case of an emergency?
___	___	Do you know what to do if you lose a camper?
___	___	Do you know what to do if a camper gets hurt?
___	___	If you allow campers to have knives, hatchets, or hand saws, are they closely supervised?
___	___	Are camp games well supervised and refereed?
___	___	Do you prevent unnecessary roughness in games?
___	___	Are campers not allowed to do an unauthorized, somewhat risky activity?
___	___	Is there anything laying around on the ground that is potential trouble (nails, boards, glass, trash)?

____ ____	Do you not allow running on slippery or rough ground?
____ ____	For special activities like horseback riding, archery, and riflery, do you require that all the safety procedures be followed?
____ ____	Are your campers carefully supervised in the craft shop if using knives or hot objects?

Hikes, Cookouts, and Campouts

**Okay   Needs
              Help**

____ ____	Do you check to be sure each camper is properly equipped for the camp-out? Have a checklist?
____ ____	Is there a first-aid kit with burn medication?
____ ____	Do you have fire fighting equipment (water,rake)?
____ ____	Is the fire protected?
____ ____	Are all burning sticks kept IN the fire?
____ ____	On hikes, have you taught them how to protect their eyes from low twigs and brush?
____ ____	For out-of-camp or woodland hikes, do you require that no camper go ahead of the lead counselor or fall behind the rear counselor?

___   ___   Can you recognize poisonous plants?

Waterfront

**Okay   Needs
        Help**

___   ___   Do you allow swimming ONLY with a
                 lifeguard there?
___   ___   Do you ALSO watch the campers?
___   ___   Do you not allow overloading of boats?
___   ___   Do you require every boater to wear a
                 lifejacket?
___   ___   Do you help keep campers INSIDE the
                 boating area?
___   ___   Do you allow boating only WITH proper
                 supervision?

Health

**Okay   Needs
        Help**

___   ___   Are you alert to signs of colds and
                 illnesses?
___   ___   Can you keep their feet dry in cool
                 weather?

___	___	Can campers be kept warm enough at night?
___	___	Do you watch for a balanced nutritional meal (what they actually eat)?
___	___	Do you control how much candy and pop is eaten at the snack shack?
___	___	When changing into swim suits, do you casually check for signs of a rash (communicable disease) or signs of child abuse? Do you report this to the Nurse?
___	___	Do you maintain your own personal hygiene with showers, deodorant and so forth?
___	___	Do you get adequate rest, eat nutritional food, and avoid the sugars, starches, and oily foods?

24 How to Help Write a Book

This book is not yet complete. I would like your ideas. Take any chapter and add the refinements you have made.

Then add whole chapters of other camp counselor skills you have learned.

Here is how to do it, so that I can use it:

- Send only ideas, methods and techniques that you have used repeatedly with success.

- Send all your ideas in clear handwriting or double-spaced, type-written form.

- All submissions become the property of McElroy Publishing. Please do not copy from other books. If we use your idea, your name will appear with your entry in the newly revised book.

- Clearly label each entry with your full name, address, phone number, name of your camp, and the number of weeks your idea was used. If you have other background in camping or in college training, please include that information as well.

- Send this to: **McElroy Publishing, P.O. Box 488, Shirley, MA 01464.** From this same address, more of these books can be ordered.

Index

Order Form

If you would like more copies of this book, please tear out this order form and enclose it with a check made out to the MCELROY PUBLISHING. Alternatively, you may call toll free 1-800-225-0682 to order direct. All orders are backed by an unconditional one-year return privilege. Please inquire, if interested, about the quantity discount schedule.

Quantity	Item	Unit Price	Total
	How To Be A Great Camp Counselor	$12.95	
	The Camp Counselor's Handbook of Over 90 Games And Activities Just For Rainy Days	$5.95	

U. S. Shipping Add $4.50/unit	Subtotal	
Canadian Shipping Add $7.50/unit	Shipping	
Overseas Shipping Add $12.00/unit	Total	

Name		
Camp/Company		
Address		
City	State	Zip
Phone ( ) —		

McElroy Publishing
27-33 Fredonian Street
P.O. Box 488
Shirley, MA 01464

Order Form

If you would like more copies of this book, please tear out this order form and enclose it with a check made out to the MCELROY PUBLISHING. Alternatively, you may call toll free 1-800-225-0682 to order direct. All orders are backed by an unconditional one-year return privilege. Please inquire, if interested, about the quantity discount schedule.

Quantity	Item	Unit Price	Total
	How To Be A Great Camp Counselor	$12.95	
	The Camp Counselor's Handbook of Over 90 Games And Activities Just For Rainy Days	$5.95	

U. S. Shipping Add $4.50/unit	Subtotal	
Canadian Shipping Add $7.50/unit	Shipping	
Overseas Shipping Add $12.00/unit	Total	

Name			
Camp/Company			
Address			
City	State	Zip	
Phone ( ) —			

McElroy Publishing
27-33 Fredonian Street
P.O. Box 488
Shirley, MA 01464